PEGGY HUTCHINSON'S HOME-MADE WINE SECRETS

PEGGY HUTCHINSON'S
HOME-MADE WINE SECRETS

LONDON
W. FOULSHAM & CO. LTD.
NEW YORK · TORONTO · CAPE TOWN · SYDNEY

MADE IN GREAT BRITAIN.
PRINTED BY C. TINLING & CO. LTD., LIVERPOOL, LONDON AND PRESCOT.

PREFACE

The recipes in this book were originally compiled in the days of plenty before the Second World War. Times have changed; some of the ingredients are no longer easy to obtain, and prices have increased. Yet when I came to revise the book I found that it needed less alteration than I had feared. Apart from a few minor alterations I was able to leave the recipes in their original form. All that I have had to rewrite is the introductory chapter, " General Hints on Wine Making." I have modified this to take into account the changed conditions, and at the end of it will be found advice on the use of substitutes for ingredients that are not easily obtainable.

The purpose of the book remains the same as when it was written. My aim has been true thrift—namely, getting the best from the means within our hand. The nation's wine bill to foreign countries is larger than ever, and I contend that the British housewife can, with care, make equally good wines in small or large quantities. Prices of ingredients have certainly increased—but the rise in the retail prices of imported wines (now very heavily taxed) is far greater in proportion, so that many people have come to regard wines as luxuries beyond their means. There is no need for this attitude if they will make their own wines. By this means they can revive the traditional old English hospitality, when wine and cake were served to all callers, and housewives treasured their particular recipes and vied with one another in the excellency of their brews.

I have made all these wines and will continue to experiment, and I shall give gladly of my knowledge to any sister in difficulties, should she write to me enclosing a stamped addressed envelope.

PEGGY HUTCHINSON

THE HALL,
BYERS GREEN,
VIA SPENNYMOOR,
CO. DURHAM.

CONTENTS

The Recipes are arranged Alphabetically.

HOME-MADE WINE SECRETS

GENERAL HINTS ON WINE MAKING

The word "wine" conjures up in one's mind a vision of vats, barrels, and cool cellars, all of which make wine making seem a very elaborate undertaking.   But wine making in the home is easy.   With inexpensive materials, ordinary kitchen equipment, and very little trouble, the average housewife can make good, fine English wine.

The garden and hedgerow provide a multitude of fragrant blooms and berries that will yield a gallon of delightful wine for less than the price of a single bottle of the cheapest wine in the shops.   The range of types and flavours is wide and many of the ingredients cost nothing at all.

The most important ingredient of all is *time*, and that costs nothing but patience.   For wine makes itself.

The main qualities to aim at in wine making are flavour, body, clearness, and colour.   There are a number of different methods of wine making, and these can be put under four general headings :

(1) The cold water method.
(2) The boiling water and boiling method.
(3) The pure juice method.
(4) The diluted juice method.

The recipes in this book include examples of all of these methods.   I have given the most suitable method for each wine.

7

UTENSILS

When you first start wine making there is no reason why you should not simply use whatever utensils you have at hand, and make just half a gallon.

When that has turned out a success, you will probably decide that it is no more trouble to make two gallons; and all you will need for this will be vessels large enough to ferment and mature the brew. Even then you will not have to spend a great deal of money, and the things you buy will soon pay for themselves.

First of all, get a big jar of the kind that was formerly used in farmhouses to hold cream. The 1½-gallon or 2-gallon size will be most suitable.

The second stage of the process requires the " grey hen " or gallon stone jar.

Some people are lucky enough to have a small barrel, and certainly if you can make one or two gallons of wine, there is no reason why you should not make six. But don't take the inside of the barrel too much for granted. Wood holds flavour for a long time, and it is wise to make very sure what has been in the barrel. Rum or black beer, for example, would spoil the colour in a pale, delicate wine; on the other hand, it would improve both colour and flavour in the heavy yellow and brown varieties. If you are going to make rhubarb wine, for example, there is no need to clean out the barrel.

The third stage of the process needs a large glass bottle to clear economically. A half-stone sweet bottle is excellent for the purpose.

Finally, you want new bottles and new corks.

Possession of these utensils will make wine making a pleasure; but they can all be done without, for after fermenting the brew for a week it can be put into bottles.

Whatever utensils you use, it is most important that you should keep them in good condition.

Years ago, I learned a lesson about this. I cleaned out a stone jar with boiling soda water, smelt it, and drained it and set it to get thoroughly dry. Then I filled it up with cowslip wine. Some four months later I turned it out to clear, and found it spoiled, tasting and smelling very musty.

It had to be thrown out, and I was very puzzled over the condition. To get rid of the mustiness I soaked the jar with boiling soda water for days, and then found it rattled as though it had something inside. This " something " turned out to be an old cork—practically a blue-green ball of nasty, fusty mould! Moral: soak each jar fully a week to get all off the bottom.

Never put wine in wet bottles. After washing out thoroughly with hot soda water, rinse them well in cold water and then put them in the oven and bake them until they are completely dry inside.

Don't let sediment lie at the bottom of wine bottles. This ruins the flavour. Sometimes I have poured wine over four times.

Finally, never set wine to ferment in enamel or tin bowls. You get an indescribable " tinny " flavour that is disagreeable.

INGREDIENTS

Making good wine is so simple, and requires so little in the way of ingredients. You can make strong and invigorating brews from blooms, berries, leaves, and even waste. There is a very wide range for you to choose from, and all you have to do is to make your choice.

In wines as in everything else, one man's meat is another man's poison ; and when you are making wine you must study your family's taste. On no account become a one-flavour wine maker. Suit the popular taste for sweetness, and give variety.

Caution is needed when you make up a wine recipe for yourself, and it is wise to consider carefully the distinct properties of various flowers and fruits, keeping a watchful eye on the strength of flavour.

As a rule you can class flowers up generally in your mind. Any strong-smelling flower will yield good results, excepting poppies and deadly nightshade. These flowers are harmful, as most country people know.

Flower heads and petals make the choicest wine. I find the stalks too strong and harsh. I like the flower heads best as the little green that goes with them produces an exquisite greeny-yellow colour that is truly delightful in primrose and cowslip. But you must be very careful in gauging quantities, as some flowers are harsh in flavour, and so rather less bulk of flower must go to the gallon.

Berries and fruit give the best colour when taken as soon as they are ripe. Those that have been hung through sunshine and rain have lots of moisture, but no colour and no flavour. All wines from such things as plums and brambles are nicer when leaning to red, and this is only obtained by keeping a wary eye on the season.

Some fascinating mixtures can be got by putting a later fruit to an earlier variety, or by putting two or several together, after making or in the making.

Fruit and flowers must never be wet with either rain or dew when used. Such wetness causes a mildew taste and a greeny-blue mould to rise both in the jar and afterwards in the bottle. If fruit is wet when gathered, boil it in the water for twenty minutes.

Certain shrubs and herbs make fine, sparkling wine, such as rosemary, balm, mint and sage, when newly sprouted in the spring. After that they are too strong and make up bitterly.

Dried fruits also make fine wine, and are economical, as the fruit can be eaten; for there is no mashing done in the tub, only the liquor being fermented.

Almost everything can be made into good wine, including cabbage, turnips, and waste. Waste is an excellent wine maker—by this I mean orange skins and halves of lemons after being squeezed; apple cores and peelings, and windfall and bad apples (those with brown patches on them); small potatoes; lettuce and spinach leaves (the coarse ones); the hard blackberries, the poor-quality gooseberries and currants; little wizened, tough carrots, beets, and parsnips; unripened grapes from a cold greenhouse, and even the leaves of grape-vines and the oak, and spring leaf-buds from the elder and bramble. All of these will make a good, nourishing brew. So will left-overs from meals—a cupful of rice pudding, a cupful of mashed potatoes, a few sultanas and two quarts of water with $1\frac{1}{2}$ lb. of golden syrup will make a wine fit for a king ! Marrow leaves and peelings and seeds, little tomatoes, mint, and the cores and skins of pears left when bottling fruit, all make excellent strong, drinkable wines. The list is almost endless.

ADDITIONAL INGREDIENTS

Seasoned drinkers like to feel a tingling heat in their fingers and toes. You can get a whisky-like quality in heat by adding whole cloves, whole ginger, peppercorns, or mustard seeds ; you must wash them before adding. For a time you have the clove, ginger, pepper or mustard flavour ; but it goes as the wine is kept, leaving only the tingling heat in the brew. Ginger in the bottle keeps the wine and improves its heat every day. Allow not more than $\frac{1}{4}$ lb. to the gallon ; 1 oz. is the wiser amount.

I find that whole cloves are better than ground cloves, which give a too pronounced taste. Whole cloves give heat with only a slight flavour, and in certain wines and syrups this is valuable for use as a nightcap for colds. A very fine wine is made solely with one ounce of cloves.

I do not advise stick cinnamon to flavour.

Malt, hops, barley, and wheat are all powerful additions to the brew, but these can be just as powerful an agent for ill in the hands of ignorance, for the bitterness of too many hops has to be tasted before it can be believed. Barley needs to be used with care. Barley wine has no harshness in making —it has a smooth, milk-like quality—but must be taken with care for it is deceptively mild to taste. The barley such as used to be ground for pigs and fed whole to hens cannot be obtained now, so you must be satisfied with pearl barley— that is, dressed barley from the shops.

There are other things that can be added that will make a big improvement, such as grape leaves, Indian corn, raisins,

sultanas, and the peelings of oranges, lemons, and apples.
Banana skins also give a fine flavour.

Before you start experimenting, however, first learn to make
wine from the recipes as I have given them. If you throw
a recipe out of balance you may find that you have wasted
your ingredients.

MAKING THE WINE

If once you can fix a general rule in your head for wines,
light, medium, and heavy, irrespective of kind, you will see
just how easy a brew is to put together.

For a light wine, use 3 lb. to 4 lb. of fruit and one quart
of petals to the gallon.

For a medium flower wine, half a gallon of heads and 6 lb.
of fruit to the gallon will make a good bouquet and give
strength.

For a heavy fruit wine, half a gallon of fruit to one gallon
of water, even a gallon to a gallon, will make a good, rich
brew. For extra heaviness use half a gallon of water to
one gallon of fruit.

Decide just the kind you want, and work accordingly.

To stir, mash and squeeze the fruit, I use my hand. This
method is safer, cutting out all possibility of leaving the spoon
resting at the side while you move something to make room
on the shelf, and later find that the spoon slipped under the
fruit and has been in the brew for days, completely spoiling
the fine flavour the wine ought to have had.

Good colour is important. Bear in mind that boiling
water will set a red but rob a yellow. Boiling water will
rob certain kinds of wine of all distinctive properties, scent
as well as colour, whereas cold water will preserve both.

Common sense and seasonal considerations must be taken
into calculation. The period of mashing depends on the
weather, for on hot, muggy days the fruits mould in the
mash. All mould should be taken off daily, and any sign
of deterioration of fruit, leaf or flower is a signal for its
removal. It is often quite easy to squeeze out the offending

ingredient without disturbing the whole brew. On the other hand, never remove fruit or flower until you have got every particle of juice and flavour out of it, even if the recipe says only " stand ten days ". If the mash is very fresh, I squeeze and push the fruit down for eighteen days and more, until I feel absolutely sure that I have got all the goodness into the liquor.

Some seasons the fruit is very soft, and quickly dissolves into the liquid ; but very dry years usually mean that fruits like plums and cherries take three days to swell with the water. Flowerlets float on top and are easily skimmed off if you think they have given all their flavour.

Vine leaves must not be left in until they rot, although one summer I had them mixed with gooseberries for over a month.

Keep a book and write down the date of each brew and all the peculiarities it developed in the making, and this will guide you in the future and finally become invaluable. Using the same fruit and the same recipe gives different results in different years. A wet season will give a syrupy thickness that will clear up with time and make a heavy " body ". A fine, dry year gives a full-flavoured thin wine of beautiful colour—and a multitude of beetles that take a lot of shaking off the flowers before wetting !

Making wine is like throwing a ball—you take good aim and throw straight, and yet the minute the ball leaves your hand it starts a career of its own, and you simply have to stand by and watch it take its course. That is the way of wine.

Some of my plum port has become a thin, red ruby wine ; another brew has been a heavy red wine ; and yet a third has turned out the colour and taste of real port. I am still trying to decide which I like best. Yet the same kind of plum and the same method were used for all of them. This has happened time and time again, and it is one of the things that makes wine making so fascinating. I welcome this variety, for each of the brews has its own special virtues and is good to drink.

15

STRAINING LIQUIDS

Straining liquids properly is most important. Use a thick cloth—either two teacloths one on top of the other or two thicknesses of flannelette are good — and make a sort of three-cornered bag, fixed between two chairs over a bowl. This allows you to lift and pour with two hands—a big advantage when handling a large quantity of boiling hot liquid. Never try to hurry the straining by squeezing or stirring. That only makes a muddiness hang in the bottle. Just let the liquid run through in its own time.

A second straining—through a bag made with three thicknesses of muslin if you can get it, firmly fixed into an embroidery frame—is an advantage. It may save a lot of wine when the final stage of clearing is reached—for a well-strained brew means that you get a clear liquid quickly, without much loss with the sediment when the brew clears itself.

FERMENTATION

Fermentation is the process that really makes the wine, and this does not call for any work on your part. All you have to do is to let the brew ferment in the conditions it needs.

Always cover the fermenting jar with a thick cloth or blanket. A brew gone vinegary usually means that you did not keep it covered when it was fermenting, to exclude the air.

Wine ferments quietly for two or three months after it is bottled. This is really a process of maturing, and it is best done in bulk in a grey hen. The brew then gathers a fuller and finer bouquet. Here you can see the importance of the most necessary ingredient in making wine—time.

The process of fermentation is quite easy to understand. On the outside of fruits like grapes, currants, and brambles, there is a blush called *bloom*. This is a natural yeast, so that mashed fruit will ferment (in the right temperature) without a single thing being added. However, in making over 600 gallons of wine, I have found that the addition of yeast and sugar or other sweetening makes a strong spirit content in the wine, and gives it the "something" that makes you warm and "happy", and that is why I advise these additions in the recipes.

Some wines mature more quickly than others, a change taking place in the bottle every hour. You will see tiny little bubbles come up and break on the surface; that is quiet fermentation, and it goes on for months. It is this "working" that refines the wine and makes it so delicious in the finished bottle. If you find that your wine has no movement, then it is in too cold a place. It will not spoil, but it will stand still and not improve until it gets into a warmer temperature. So generally speaking, you must ferment in the kitchen, or a room where there is a fire on daily, or in summertime. Don't let the brew fret, or, in other words, have a very slow fermentation. Hasten the process by moving the jar into a warmer position. Don't expect good fermentation, especially if no yeast is used, unless the temperature is sufficient. It takes a living-room temperature to set it going.

THE USE OF SUGAR

The addition of sugar or other sweetening gives wines a heady spirit content, but it makes them take longer to mature into that pleasing mellowness which is the keynote to quality.

Generally speaking, I have found that most brews need 4 lb. of sugar to the gallon. However, the need varies with the wine. Petals, for example, have no acidity and therefore need less (3 lb. is sufficient); but in a heavy wine of, say, 6 lb. fruit to the gallon, 4½ lb. of sugar will be needed. Pure juice such as gooseberry requires 6 lb. or more of sugar—and takes six years to mature.

Never use cheap sugar or the Scotch brown. Both mean extra loss in the clearing stage. It is far better to add a good sugar at the beginning, when both colour and flavour will gain by your selection.

For the delightful pale wines, such as primrose and cowslip, I advise white sugar. Best demerara will not help these;

on the contrary, it spoils the fine, faint hint of green that should tinge the yellow. For brandy cocktail, too, white sugar is best. But the best demerara definitely does help the heavy yellow kinds, like lemon, rhubarb, and all the port-like brews.

Pink sugar will not help ports at all, and should only be used for the very delicate kinds.

Dark barley sugar will help the colour. Some people add burnt sugar and black " spanish ", but these must be used with the greatest caution. Always be very careful about making additions of any kind, for they may interfere with the flavour and ruin your wine.

Thick wine is made by boiling the sugar into the water for thirty minutes or an hour. You boil the quantity down, and when it is lukewarm, add yeast. In summers when insects are in the fruit this is the best method to use with plums, apples, and brambles.

THE USE OF YEAST

Yeast is added to some brews, not to make it ferment—for in the right temperature it will ferment with sugar and water, or even with water alone—but to help to develop the spirit content of the wine. It is not essential ; and in the most delicate wines you get a finer, fuller flavour, more true to kind, without using yeast. At first the spirit content suffers, but it gathers with time. A quieter fermentation simply means that you have to keep the wine a little longer in the bottle to get a full, mature bouquet.

One ounce of yeast, or even half an ounce, to the gallon is the right quantity. The usual method of using it is to mix it to a spreadable paste and then spread it over a piece of toast, which is floated on top of the wine. You can tone down the exuberance in the wine by placing the toast with the yeast side to the brew for only half the time of the fer-mentation, then turning the toast so that the goodness goes chiefly from the bread.

Yeast may also be crumbled and sprinkled over the brew

16

without toast or bread; but the brew must be cold or luke-warm, and this should be done only in certain recipes.

"TRICKS OF THE TRADE"

There are many "tricks of the trade" in wine making, and one of the most important things to remember is that wine should never be thrown away just because it tastes sour and crabbed.

I once made some redcurrant wine, and tasted the brew after a few months. It was very sour and crabbed—and, foolishly, I poured it out. By luck I overlooked two bottles, and found them three years later. The wine proved to be delightful! That was a lesson to me in the futility of trying to make wine without the most necessary ingredient—time.

The point is that some wines mature more quickly than others, and a change takes place every three months. Often a brew develops a crabbed sourness at three months when it is busy developing "body". Don't throw it out as soured on the impulse of the moment. It only needs time to break up the crabbedness and bring out the fullness in flavour and body. At six months the flavour will probably be harsh with the sourness gone, and at twelve months there will be a matured brew in the bottle.

Sometimes the breaking up of the crabbedness can be helped with the addition of a little dark barley sugar to the brew. For example, elder flower made with golden syrup at times develops a raw bite; a little crushed barley sugar or brown toffee ($\frac{1}{2}$ lb. to the gallon) improves both the colour and taste.

I find that some seasons there is an extra acidity content in the wine, and that it gives a tremendous "grip" in the taste which is not altogether agreeable to the general palate. To counteract this fault I pull $\frac{1}{4}$ lb. of large raisins apart and add to the bulk, this quantity to a gallon; but more or less can be added according to the strength of the "grip" in taste. Where I feel that the harshness is due to a lack of sweetness owing to all the sugar being converted into spirit.

I add ¼ lb. or more (as needed) of brown sugar candy or barley sugar, but not till the wine is six months old. This causes a mild fermentation, so the wine must not be corked too closely. But remember that all wine is harsh for the first six months and needs keeping, to justify the colour, clearness, and flavour. Saccharine is valuable in breaking up crabbedness, but it is a thing to be used with great care. Do not add more than one or two saccharines to the pint; one and a half is the best measurement. Only use when the wine has been kept over a time. I often use it in bramble wine. Always crush the saccharine before adding.

According to the harshness of the wine, you may also have to heat a little wine and stir into it ½ lb. or 1 lb. of syrup, then adding this to the whole and stirring to mix it in. Then cork, and leave for a month in a warm place. When you add extra sweetening of any kind, always let the wine stand for one, two, or three months in a warm place. Then taste it, and you will see how it has improved to a fine, drinkable quality.

When rhubarb wine is too sharp of acidity, add two large raisins to each bottle. This mellows it down beautifully.

A brew that remains stultifyingly sweet, on the other hand, needs some addition to turn that sweetness into a fine spirit content. One two-inch-thick slice of bread put in and left in a gallon for a week will make a surprising difference.

CLEARING

I find it a waste of time trying to clear wine while it is still fermenting. This can easily be seen when you knock the bottle on the shelf. Tiny air bubbles run up the wine, as they do in lemonade.

There are three methods of getting your wines beautifully clear and sparkling. First of all, you can use eggshells. Two or three to the gallon is usually the right number, unless you want to make a completely colourless brew. For example, you can make a clear, strong white brandy-like brew by adding four or more eggshells to a gallon of rhubarb wine, thus taking out every vestige of colour. Eggshells do not interfere with the flavour of the wine, but leave a small lime content.

It is most important to use only eggshells that are fresh. If they are not fresh, they will have a flavour ; and, of course, the shell of an egg that has been in waterglass would ruin the brew, for waterglass is strong washing soda.

The second method of clearing is by beating the white of an egg into it. This should be used only in obstinate cases, when you want to hurry away the milky appearance.

The third method is with isinglass, and this is the easiest of the three. Some people use it wet, others dry ; I like it dry, as I believe this gives more sparkle to the finished brew.

I use large sweet bottles for the business. I fill them up and add to each a big pinch of isinglass—that is, a piece about the size of a golf-ball. Isinglass can be bought by the ounce. It is a light, hair-like substance, and you get a lot for an ounce. Soon you will see it begin to work up and down in the wine and swell, clearing the gross and reducing it to a sediment. Soon you will have crystal-clear wine on top, and this must be poured into clean bottles.

In clearing wine there is a certain amount of waste—although this is less if the brew was well strained—as you have to clear off the " bottoms " all the way. If left in, these rob the wine of much of its flavour.

CORKING

If possible, always use new corks. Beware of screw-stoppered bottles, for they are liable to go off " bang," making a dreadful mess with broken glass, and liquor will be spattered over the walls. Corks are safer, as they will blow out and can be replaced without much loss and upset. Do not worry about corks being blown out. This is bound to happen sometimes. But if you find the corks blowing out one after another, it is a sign that you have got the wine in too warm a place. So move it somewhere cooler—although not too cool to stop the fermentation.

You will notice throughout the recipes that you are advised to cork lightly at first. You must do this. If you cork too tightly, you will have a burst bottle, which is dangerous and messy—and your wine will be lost. Never seal your corks until you are sure that all violent fermentation has ceased. When this happens, you can cork tightly and seal.

SUBSTITUTES

Since I first wrote this book, some of the ingredients have become rationed or difficult to obtain, and in the last few years I have been experimenting with substitutes.

I have found that good golden syrup or honey can be used instead of sugar. The quantity to be used depends on the wine, but in general golden syrup should be the same as for sugar. Honey is dear, and must be treated with respect. If too much is used you get a *flavour* and a potent brew which gives you a violent headache for days.

When I wrote this book wheat and barley were plentiful and cost only about a penny a pint. Now times have changed, and substitutes may be required. I have found that the best substitute for wheat is white bread. Use one two-inch slice of bread to a gallon. An alternative is wheat flakes or Shredded Wheat. Two Shedded Wheat cakes may be used for 1 lb. of wheat.

Barley may be used instead of wheat in certain recipes, but remember that it makes the wine mature more quickly. On no account use both barley and wheat, or you will throw the recipe out of balance.

You can boil pearl barley or rice in water for thirty to forty minutes, and then strain out and use the barley or rice for puddings. The water can be made into any kind of wine, and will give a potent brew.

Lemons, oranges, and sultanas are obtainable. Sultanas can be used instead of raisins. Dates and other dried fruits are admissible.

RECIPES FOR WINES

ALMOND WINE (1)

Ingredients :

1½ ozs. bitter almonds
1 lb. raisins
3 lbs. sugar
1 gallon water
3 lemons
1 oz. yeast ; 1 slice of toast

Method :

1. Chop the almonds and raisins and boil gently in the water for an hour, then strain and make the liquid up to one gallon.

2. Add the sugar and stir it away, then the juice and rind of lemons and when lukewarm add the yeast spread on toast. Leave to ferment 14 days.

3. Then strain and bottle.

ALMOND WINE (2)

Ingredients :

4 lbs. rhubarb
1 lemon
3½ lbs. sugar
¼ lb. sultanas
2 large teaspoonfuls almond essence
½ oz. yeast on large slice toast

Method :

1. Cut the rhubarb up small, cover with the water and stand 14 days, stirring and squeezing every day. Then squeeze the rhubarb pulp out and throw it away.

2. Add to the liquid the sugar, almond essence, chopped lemon, sultanas and yeast spread on both sides of the toast. Stand to ferment 14 days.

3. Then skim, strain and bottle. Keep 12 months.

APPLE AND BLAEBERRY[1] WINE

Ingredients :

>4 lbs. apples (windfalls will do, but they must be clean
>4 lbs. blaeberries
>4 lbs. sugar
>½ lb. raisins
>1 gallon water

Method :

1. Cut up the apples (do not peel or core) and put them with ½ gallon of cold water. Squeeze and stir every day for 8 days, then strain.

2. Cover the blaeberries with cold water and stir and squeeze for 4 days until all the juice is in the liquid, then strain.

3. Add the liquids together. Add the chopped raisins and sugar and stir until the sugar is dissolved. Let it ferment 20 days, then skim, strain and bottle. Keep 12 months.

APPLE PORT
(Very rich and strong)

Ingredients :

>8 lbs. apples
>4½ lbs. sugar
>6 lbs. blaeberries
>1 gallon water

Method :

1. Cut the apples up small and place in the cold water (do not peel, and leave any brown patches on). Break up with the hands every day for 14 days, then strain all pulp out of the liquid.

2. Put the sugar in and stir until it is dissolved then add the blaeberries and keep breaking them up into the liquid every day for 8 days. Then strain and squeeze all moisture from the pulp before throwing it away.

3. Leave the liquid to stand for 3 weeks, then skim and bottle. Keep 12 months.

[1] The Scottish name for Bilberry or Whortleberry.

APPLE SHERRY

Ingredients :

> 2 lbs. apricots (dried)
> 6 lbs. apples (windfalls will do
> 1 gallon water
> 1 lb. raisins
> 1 cake shredded wheat
> 3½ lbs. sugar

Method :

1. Boil the apricots in the water until very tender, then strain the liquid off and use the apricots as food.

2. Cut up the apples (leaving skin and brown patches on) and pour the apricot liquid over. Squeeze and mash every day for 14 days, then strain all pulp out.

3. Add the shredded wheat, chopped raisins and sugar and leave to ferment 21 days.

4. Then skim, strain and bottle. Keep 12 months.

APPLE WINE

Ingredients :

> 8 lbs. bruised apples
> ½ lb. sultanas
> ¼ lb. barley
> 1 gallon water
> 3½ lbs. brown sugar

Method :

1. Cut the apples into small pieces. Add the barley and sultanas and cover with cold water. Stir and squeeze the apples every day for a month, then strain.

2. Add the sugar and stir until dissolved, and leave in a warm place 21 days to ferment. Then skim and bottle, corking loosely until all fermentation ceases. At 9 months this was a strong sparkling wine.

APRICOT WINE (1)

Ingredients :

> 6 lbs. apricots
> 1 gallon water
> 4 lbs. sugar

Method :

1. Cover the apricots with water and squeeze them daily for 10 days then strain, taking care to get all the moisture from the pulp before throwing it away.

2. Add the sugar and stir until it is dissolved, then stand in a warm place to ferment for 16 days. Then skim and bottle.

APRICOT WINE (2)

Ingredients :

> 4 lbs. apricots
> 1 gallon water
> 1 lb. raisins
> 4 lbs. sugar
> 1 lb. wheat
> 1 oz. yeast

Method :

1. Cover the apricots with cold water. Mash and stir for 10 days then strain.

2. To the liquid add the chopped raisins, sugar, wheat and yeast, sprinkled over the top. Let it ferment 21 days, then strain and bottle.

BARLEY WINE

Ingredients :

    1 lb. barley

    1 lb. raisins
    1 lb. old potatoes
    4 lbs. white sugar
    1 oz. yeast
    1 gallon water (hot but not boiling)

Method :

1. Put the barley, raisins, potatoes (not peeled and cut into small chunks), and sugar into a jar. Cover with the water.

2. Dissolve the yeast in a little warm water and add. Leave to stand 3 weeks, stirring daily.

3. Then strain and bottle, leave the corks loose for a week, then fasten more securely. Keep 6 months. A lovely golden wine.

BEETROOT WINE (1)

Ingredients :

    4 lbs. beetroot
    1 gallon water
    4 lbs. sugar
    1 lb. wheat
    1 oz. yeast

Method :

1. Boil the beetroot in the water and take it out when done. Skin it and cut in slices. Cover with vinegar for pickle.

2. Strain the water well, add the sugar and stir until it is dissolved.

3. When lukewarm add the wheat and sprinkle the yeast over the top. Let it ferment 14 days before skimming and bottling.

4. Remember to put the corks in loosely.

BEETROOT WINE (2)

Ingredients :

3 lbs. beetroot
3 lbs. parsnips
1 gallon water
3¾ lbs. sugar
¼ lb. large raisins
1 oz. yeast on a large slice of toast

Method :

1. Boil the beetroot in half the water until tender, then skin and use the beetroot.

2. Boil the parsnips in the remaining half of the water until tender. Strain and use them as a vegetable.

3. Strain the waters and add them together. Stir the sugar in and add the chopped raisins.

4. Spread the yeast on the toast and float on the top. Let it ferment 21 days then strain and bottle.

BEETROOT WINE (3)
(Hackthorpe)

Ingredients :

1 gallon water
4 lbs. beetroots
4 lbs. sugar
Juice of 3 lemons
8 cloves

Method :

1. Wash the beetroot and cut it up quickly into the water and boil 20 minutes, then strain.

2. Add the sugar and lemon juice while the liquid is hot. Stir the sugar away, add the cloves and leave to ferment for 3 weeks.

3. Then skim, strain and bottle. A glass of rum can be added if liked, but very good without it.

BLACK CHERRY WINE

Ingredients :

> 6 lbs. black cherries
> 1 gallon boiling water
> ½ lb. sultanas
> 3½ lbs. sugar
> 1 oz. yeast; a large slice toast

Method :

1. Put the cherries in a bowl and pour the boiling water over. Next day break up with your hand all the fruit, add the chopped sultanas, sugar and yeast spread on both sides of the toast. Leave for 14 days, stirring daily.

2. Then strain all pulp out and squeeze all moisture from it.

3. Leave the liquid 14 days then bottle it.

BLACKCURRANT WINE

Ingredients :

> 1 gallon blackcurrants
> 1 gallon water
> 4 lbs. sugar
> 1 oz. yeast
> 2 slices of toast

Method :

1. Put the currants and water together and bring slowly to the boil and simmer until all the goodness is in the water (about 20 minutes). Then strain.

2. Put the sugar and 1 slice of slightly toasted bread into a bowl. Pour the boiling blackcurrant liquid over and stir until the sugar is dissolved.

3. When lukewarm add the yeast spread on the remaining slice of toast and ferment 14 days. Then strain and bottle, corking loosely. Keep 1 or 2 years.

BLAEBERRY [1] WINE

Ingredients :

- 1 gallon blaeberries
- 1 gallon cold water
- 4 lbs. sugar
- 1 oz. yeast
- 1 large slice of toast

Method :

1. Put the blaeberries into the cold water and stir and mash for 6 days, then strain.

2. Into the liquid put the sugar and stir until it is dissolved. Then spread the yeast on the toast and put it into the liquid and leave in a warm place to ferment for 14 days. Skim and bottle, corking loosely until all fermentation has ceased.

BRAMBLE CLARET

Ingredients :

- 1 gallon brambles
- 1 quart sloes
- 1 gallon boiling water
- 4 lbs. sugar
- ½ oz. yeast
- 1 large slice of toast

Method :

1. Pour the boiling water over the brambles (blackberries). Leave 6 days, mashing the fruit each day.

2. Squeeze all moisture out of the fruit and throw the pulp away.

3. Add the sugar, sloes and the yeast which has been spread on toast.

4. Stir and mash the sloes every day for a fortnight, as it is fermenting.

5. Then skim and run through three thicknesses of muslin before bottling. Keep 6 months.

[1] The Scottish name for Bilberry or Whortleberry

BRAMBLE LIQUEUR (1)
(Swarland)

Ingredients :

> 9 quarts brambles
> 10 pints water
> 12 lbs. sugar

Method :

1. Boil the water and pour it over the fruit. Let it stand 7 days, squeezing and stirring daily.

2. Strain and squeeze every drop of liquid from the fruit before throwing the pulp away, then strain the liquid through a clean muslin.

3. Add the sugar to the liquid and let it ferment 7 days.

4. Then skim and bottle, corking lightly.

5. Add a little rum or brandy if liked and keep 12 months.

(These Bramble Liqueurs make a fine toddy cure for a cold.)

BRAMBLE LIQUEUR (2)

Ingredients :

> To every quart of pure bramble juice 1 lb. of white sugar
> To a gallon of juice 1 oz. white ginger, well bruised and
> 1 glass of gin

Method :

1. Put the brambles in a jar. Set the jar in a pan of boiling water over heat to draw the juice. Measure the pure juice and add the sugar. Stir until it is dissolved.

2. Put in a warm place and leave 8 days to ferment then skim and bottle.

3. This can be made in quarts, as one can gather the fruit. I portion the gin out to 2 teaspoonfuls for each quart bottle. Keep 6 months. The ginger is added 1 month before use.

BRAMBLE PORT (1)

Ingredients :

1 gallon brambles (blackberries)
1 pint sloes and 1 lb. damsons
1 gallon boiling water
4 lbs. lump sugar
½ oz. yeast
1 large slice of bread

Method :

1. Pour the boiling water over the brambles, damsons and sloes. Leave 8 days, mashing each day.

2. Strain and squeeze every drop of moisture from the fruit before throwing it away.

3. Strain the liquid through three thicknesses of muslin.

4. Add the sugar and stir until it is dissolved. Spread the yeast over the toast and place on the wine in a warm situation for 7 days to ferment.

5. Then skim and bottle. Keep 6 months.

BRAMBLE PORT (2)
(Jean's)

Ingredients :

1 gallon brambles (blackberries)
1 gallon water
To every 3 pints of liquid, 1 lb. sugar
1 glass rum (to every gallon of wine)

Method :

1. Put the brambles in a pan, cover with the water and bring to the boil. Then simmer for 10 minutes.

2. Strain, squeezing every drop of moisture from the fruit before throwing it away.

3. Run the liquid through three thicknesses of muslin.

4. Measure and put in the sugar. (You must measure the liquid and allow 1 lb. of sugar to every 3 pints.) Stir until dissolved.

5. Let it ferment 6 days in a warm place, skim and add the rum to the bulk before bottling. Keep 6 months.

Point to remember : It is quite nice without the rum.

BRAMBLE WINE (1)
(Heavy Body)

Ingredients :

>6 lbs. brambles
>1 gallon water
>3 lbs. sugar
>1 lb. wheat

Method :

1. Boil the brambles and water together for 10 minutes, then strain the skins and seeds out of the liquid.

2. Let the liquid get lukewarm. Add the sugar and wheat, stir until sugar is dissolved and leave to ferment for 14 days, skimming occasionally.

3. When the fermentation has ceased strain and cork up tightly, and keep 6 months.

BRAMBLE WINE (2)
(Gingered)

Ingredients :

>1 gallon brambles
>1 gallon boiling water
>4 lbs. sugar
>$\frac{1}{2}$ oz. essence of ginger
>$\frac{1}{2}$ oz. tartaric acid

Method :

1. Pour the brambles into the boiling water and boil 10 minutes or longer until all the goodness is in the water, then strain and squeeze all the moisture from the fruit before throwing the pulp away.

2. Put in the sugar and tartaric acid. Stir until the sugar is dissolved then set in a warm place and allow to ferment for 18 days. Take the top off once a week.

3. Skim and add the essence of ginger to the bulk before bottling. Keep 6 months or more.

BREAD CHAMPAGNE

Ingredients :

> 2 lbs. brown bread
> 2 lbs. sugar
> 1 gallon water

Method :

1. Cut the bread into slices and toast it—but on no account burn it or get it too dark brown.

2. Cover with the water, add the sugar and after sirring to dissolve the sugar put in a warm place to ferment for 21 days.

3. Then strain and bottle. Cork loosely.

This quickly matures.

BULLACE PORT (1)

Ingredients :

> 1 gallon bullace plums (See the plums are black ripe)
> 1 gallon boiling water
> 4 lbs. sugar

Method :

1. Cover the plums with boiling water and let them stand 14 days, squeezing and stirring daily.

2. Squeeze all the fruit pulp through a muslin and strain the liquid.

3. Add the sugar and stir until it is dissolved then leave to ferment 14 days.

4. Skim and strain before bottling.

This is a fruit growing wild in some parts of Yorkshire. I have seen it at Cropton and Newton-under-Roseberry and it is a cross between a plum and a sloe.

BULLACE PORT (2)
(Extra Heavy)

Ingredients :

> 1 gallon bullace plums
> 1 gallon boiling water
> 4 lbs. sugar
> 1 lb. wheat
> 1 oz. yeast
> ¼ lb. large raisins

Method :

1. Put the plums in a bowl, add the water and leave overnight.

2. Put your hand in the bowl and break and squeeze the fruit. Add the sugar, wheat and chopped raisins and stir until the sugar is dissolved.

3. Then mix the yeast with a little lukewarm water and pour that in. Leave to ferment 14 days, stirring every day.

4. Then strain and bottle.

BURNET PORT (1)

In Westmorland and Durham they make a port-like wine from Burnet, a herb which grows on a slender stalk with a purple plume, like a seed pod.

Ingredients :

> 2 quarts burnet heads
> 1 gallon boiling water
> 3 lbs. white sugar
> ½ oz. yeast on toast

Method :

1. Pour the boiling water over the burnets. Stand 3 nights, then strain and throw the pulp away.

2. Add the sugar to the liquid and boil gently for 30 minutes.

3. Stand until lukewarm, then cream the yeast and spread it over a slice of toast which you float on top of the brew.

4. Let it ferment 21 days, skimming around the toast now and then. Strain and bottle, corking lightly, until all fermentation ceases.

BURNET PORT (2)

Ingredients :

> 1 gallon burnet heads
> 1½ gallons boiling water
> 3 oranges
> 3 lemons
> 6 lb. white sugar
> ½ oz. yeast, spread on toast

Method :

1. Pour the boiling water over the burnets. Put a cloth over the dish and let them stand 24 hours, then strain.

2. Put the liquid in a pan with the oranges and lemons cut into slices and boil gently for 15 minutes. Let it cool to lukewarm.

3. Add the sugar, stir until it is dissolved. Spread the yeast on a slice of toast and float on top of the brew. Let it ferment 21 days, then skim and bottle.

CARNATION WINE

Ingredients ·

> 2 quarts " Pinks " (white)
> 1 gallon water
> 3 lbs. sugar
> 1 orange
> 1 lemon
> ½ lb. raisins
> 1 oz. yeast ; 1 slice toast

Method :

1. Put the flower heads into a bowl. Pour the boiling water over and leave for 3 days, stirring daily, then squeeze the flowers out.

2. Add the sugar, fruit in slices, chopped raisins and yeast spread on both sides of the toast. Ferment 3 weeks then strain and bottle.

" Pinks " are a common border carnation—the white kind make good wine.

CARROT WINE —

Ingredients :

    1 gallon water
    3½ lbs. sugar
    2 oranges
    2 lemons
    6 lbs. carrots
    1 oz. yeast
    1 large slice of toast

Method :

1. Wash the carrots well but do not peel. Put into the water and bring to the boil then simmer gently until the carrots are very tender. Use the carrots for food and strain the liquid.

2. Into the bowl put the sugar and sliced oranges and lemons and pour over the hot carrot water and stir until the sugar is dissolved ; then let it cool to lukewarm.

3. Spread the yeast on both sides of the slice of toast and float it in the liquid.

4. Let it ferment 14 days then skim and bottle. Keep 6 months or more.

CELERY WINE

Ingredients :

    4 lbs. celery (green and white)
    1 gallon of water
    3 lbs. Demerara sugar
    ½ oz. yeast
    1 large slice of toast

Method :

1. Cut the celery into short lengths and boil until tender. Strain the celery out and use the celery for food as a vegetable with white sauce.

2. Add the sugar and stir until it is dissolved. Spread the yeast on the toast and float on the liquid. Leave to ferment 14 days.

3. Then skim and bottle.

CHAMPAGNE

Ingredients :

> 1½ lbs. cracked maize (Indian Corn)
> 4 oranges
> 2 lemons
> 1 lb. large raisins
> 4½ lbs. sugar
> 1 gallon cold water

Method :

1. Put the maize, sugar and chopped raisins into a bowl. Cut the fruit in half and squeeze the juice in and afterwards put all the rinds in. Cover with the cold water and leave to ferment 21 days.

2. Strain, then bottle, but do not cork for a month, and then loosely.

Point to remember : Do not squeeze the fruit rinds.

CHRISTMAS WINE
(Whisky-like)

Ingredients :

> 4 potatoes (as big as the closed fist of a small lady's hand)
> 2 lbs. large raisins
> 4 lbs. brown sugar
> 1 pint wheat
> 1 gallon of hot, but not boiling, water
> 1 oz. yeast

Method :

1. Scrub, but not peel, the potatoes. Grate them into a large jar. Add the sugar, wheat and raisins pulled apart. Cover with the hot water.

2. When it cools to lukewarm scatter the dry yeast on top and leave to ferment 1 month, stirring daily. Then strain through a jelly bag without squeezing.

3. Add a large pinch of dry isinglass and let it stand another month, then pour off the clear wine and bottle.

CHERRY PORT (1)

Ingredients :

2 lbs. prunes
1 gallon black cherries
1 gallon water
4 lbs. sugar
1 slice of toast
1 oz. yeast

Method :

1. Boil the prunes in the water until very tender, then strain them out and use them for food.

2. Put the cherries into the liquid and squeeze and stir every day for 10 days. Then squeeze all liquid from the pulp which you throw away.

3. Add the sugar and stir until it dissolves. Add the yeast spread on both sides of the toast, then leave to ferment for 16 days.

4. Skim, strain and bottle.

CHERRY PORT (2)
(Very Heavy Body)

Ingredients :

2 gallons black cherries
1 gallon boiling water
1 lb. wheat
1 oz. yeast
4 lbs. Demerara sugar

Method :

1. Put the cherries in a bowl and cover them with boiling water. Squeeze and stir for 10 days then squeeze out all the pulp, getting it bone dry before throwing it away.

2. Add the wheat and sugar to the liquid and stir until the latter is dissolved. Sprinkle the yeast on top and leave it to ferment for 16 days, then skim and bottle.

I strained the wine, then put all the pulp in a bowl and squeezed it bit by bit through a coarse muslin to make sure of getting all the juice.

CHERRY-RHUBARB WINE (1)

Ingredients :

> 1 gallon of rhubarb (use the red rhubarb and leave all skin on)
> 1 gallon of water
> 3 lbs. red cherries (fresh)
> 4 lbs. sugar
> 1 lb. raisins
> ½ lb. wheat
> A good pinch of isinglass
> 1 oz. yeast
> 1 large slice of toast

Method :

1. Cut the rhubarb and cover with the cold water. Leave 14 days, then squeeze pulp out and throw it away.

2. Add the sugar, cherries, raisins and wheat, and spread the yeast on the toast. Stir up, squeezing often, and let it ferment. Add the isinglass and leave 3 weeks. Then strain and bottle, corking lightly until fermentation ceases. An unusual fine flavour.

CHERRY-RHUBARB WINE (2) (Seaham)

Cherry-rhubarb is the red early sort.

Ingredients :

> 1 gallon cherry-rhubarb
> 1 gallon boiling water
> 3 lbs. loaf sugar
> 1 lb. large raisins
> A pinch of isinglass to clear

Method :

1. Cut the rhubarb up very small and cover with the boiling water. Stand 9 days and stir daily. Strain and squeeze all the moisture from the pulp before throwing it away.

2. Add the sugar and raisins and isinglass. Put your hand in and stir the sugar away and squeeze the raisins. Stand 9 days, then strain.

3. Stand 3 weeks, skim and pour clear wine off the sediment at the bottom, then bottle.

4. A fine wine with no harsh acidity.

CIDER WINE

Ingredients :

> 7 lbs. small apples
> 3½ lbs. sugar
> 1 gallon water

Method :

1. Leave the skin on and cut the apples up. Cover with the water and leave to stand 21 days, squeezing and stirring every day, then strain.

2. Add the sugar to the liquid and stir until it is dissolved. Put the bowl in a warm place and let it ferment 3 weeks then skim and bottle, but do not cork too tightly for a time.

CLARY WINE

Ingredients :

> 1 lb. raisins
> 2 quarts clary blossom (the purple tops)
> 1 gallon water
> 3 lbs. sugar
> 1 oz. yeast

Method :

1. Boil the sugar and water together until the sugar is dissolved then pour this over the clary blossoms.

2. When lukewarm add the chopped raisins and sprinkle the yeast over the top.

3. After the first week take all the flowers out and leave the liquid with the raisins in to ferment a further 14 days, then strain and bottle.

CLOVER WINE

Ingredients :

Pick the flowers and let them dry in the sun
4 lbs. clover blooms
1 gallon water
3 lbs. sugar
2 lemons
2 oranges
1 oz. ginger
1 oz. yeast

Method :

1. Put the flowers, water, sugar and sliced fruit into a pan. Add the well bruised ginger and bring to the boil and simmer gently for half an hour, then strain.

2. When the liquid has cooled to lukewarm add the yeast and ferment for 14 days, then skim, strain and bottle.

CLOVE WINE

Ingredients :

1 oz. cloves
1 gallon water
1 oz. bruised ginger
1 Seville orange
3 lemons
3 lbs. Demerara sugar
1 oz. yeast ; 1 slice toast

Method :

1. Thinly peel the yellow rind from the orange and lemons and put in a muslin bag with the ginger and cloves. Put in the water and simmer gently for 1 hour.

2. Put the sugar in a bowl with the sliced orange and lemons, pour the boiling liquid over (take the bag out), stir until the sugar is dissolved and leave till lukewarm.

3. Spread the yeast on toast and float on top and leave to ferment 10 days.

4. Then skim and bottle and it is ready for use almost immediately.

COLTSFOOT WINE (1)

Ingredients :

> 3 quarts coltsfoot flowers (these must be dried in the
> sun)
> 1 pint dandelion leaves
> 1 gallon water
> 3¼ lbs. sugar
> ½ lb. raisins
> The yellow rind of 3 lemons

Method :

1. Boil the flowers, leaves and water together for 20 minutes then strain.

2. Into a bowl put rind of the lemons (don't add the juice), sugar and chopped raisins and allow to ferment for 21 days then strain.

3. Stand 14 days before bottling.

COLTSFOOT WINE (2)

Ingredients :

> 1 gallon water
> 3 pints coltsfoot flowers
> 3 lbs. sugar
> 2 oranges
> 2 lemons
> 1 oz. yeast ; 1 slice toast

Method :

1. Put the flowers and sliced fruit in a bowl.

2. Boil the sugar and water together and pour over the flowers and fruit.

3. When cool add the yeast spread on both sides of the toast and leave to ferment for 21 days.

4. Then strain and bottle.

COLTSFOOT WINE (3)
(Foalsfoot in the North)

Ingredients :

½ gallon yellow flowers
1 gallon water
1 lb. raisins
1 orange
1 lemon
3 lbs. sugar
1 oz. yeast : 1 slice toast

Method :

1. Begin by drying the flowers on a clean tray.

2. Boil the water and sugar together until the latter is melted.

3. In a bowl put the chopped raisins, sliced lemon and orange and the coltsfoot flowers, and pour the boiling water over.

4. Leave all together until lukewarm then spread the yeast on both sides of the toast and float it in the liquid part. Leave for 7 days then strain and bottle.

COWSLIP WINE (1)

Ingredients :

1 gallon cowslip flower heads
1 gallon cold water
4 lbs. sugar
Pinch of isinglass

Method :

1. Pour the water over the cowslip flowers. Use all the heads but not the fleshy stalks. Leave 15 days so that the water gathers all the fragrance and colour. Then squeeze the flowers out (but if the flowers go bad before that time take them out).

2. Stir the sugar away in the liquid, add a pinch of isinglass and set in a warm place to ferment. Let it ferment 14 days then skim and bottle. At 12 months this is a fine, strong, snappy, delicate greeny-yellow wine.

COWSLIP WINE (2)

Ingredients :

> 4 quarts cowslip flowers
> 4 quarts water
> 3 lbs. white sugar
> 1 oz. yeast
> Juice and finely grated rind of one lemon and one orange
> 1 glass brandy

Method :

1. Boil the water and sugar together for 30 minutes, skimming when necessary. When boiling pour over the orange and lemon in a bowl.

2. Leave to cool then stir in the creamed yeast and cowslip flowers.

3. Cover with a cloth and leave 48 hours, then strain.

4. Stand 14 days then skim and add the brandy before bottling.

CRAB APPLE PORT

Ingredients :

> 1 gallon crab apples
> ½ gallon brambles
> 1 gallon boiling water
> 3½ lbs. sugar
> 1 lb. raisins
> 1 oz. yeast ; a large slice toast

Method :

1. Put the crab apples and brambles in a bowl, pour the boiling water over. Stir and mash and squeeze for 14 days then strain and throw the pulp away.

2. Into the liquid add the sugar, chopped raisins and yeast spread on toast. Let it ferment 14 days.

3. Then skim and bottle. Keep 6 months.

CRAB APPLE WINE (1)

Ingredients :

1 gallon crab apples
3 lbs. brown sugar
1 gallon water

Method :

1. Cover the crab apples with the water and after 2 or 3 days when they are well soaked break up with the hand to mush.

2. Leave 21 days, stirring daily, then strain the pulp out.

3. Add the sugar and stir until dissolved. Leave to ferment in a warm place 21 days, then skim and bottle.

4. This is a very " fresh " wine so leave the corks loose for a time.

CRAB APPLE WINE (2)

Ingredients :

1 gallon crab apples
1 gallon cold water
3 lbs. sugar
1 lb. raisins
1 lb. wheat
1 oz. yeast

Method :

1. Cover the crab apples with water and after 2 or 3 days when they are swollen and soft, break them up with the hand to mush.

2. Leave 21 days, stirring daily, then strain.

3. To the liquid add the sugar, chopped raisins and wheat, then sprinkle the yeast on top. Leave to ferment 21 days, then skim and bottle.

4. This is a fine, sharp wine.

CRANBERRY WINE (1)

Ingredients :

> 6 lbs. cranberries
> 1 gallon water
> 4 lbs. white sugar

Method :

1. Pour the boiling water over the cranberries and add the sugar. Squeeze the fruit and stir every day for 8 days, then squeeze out the pulp, and squeeze it bit by bit through muslin until the pulp is dry.

2. Leave the liquid to stand 14 more days before straining and bottling.

CRANBERRY WINE (2)

Ingredients :

> 2 lbs. raisins
> 1 gallon cranberries
> 1 gallon water
> 3½ lbs. white sugar
> A large slice toast ; ½ oz. yeast

Method :

1. Boil the water and pour it over the cranberries. Mash them daily with the hand for 6 days then strain, squeezing all the moisture from the pulp before throwing it away.

2. Add the chopped raisins, sugar and toast (cut up in squares) to the liquid and stir until the sugar is dissolved.

3. Then add the yeast by sprinkling it over the top and leave for 16 days to ferment.

4. Then skim, strain and bottle.

CURRANT PORT —

Ingredients :

4 lbs. currants (dried fruit such as is put in a fruit loaf)
1 gallon of water
3½ lbs. sugar
1 lb. wheat
1 oz. yeast

Method :

1. Boil the currants in the water for 30 minutes, then stand to cool. Add the sugar, stir it away and break up the currants.

2. When lukewarm add the wheat and yeast which has been dissolved in a little warm water.

3. Stir and squeeze daily for 21 days then strain and bottle. Keep 1 year.

DAISY WINE

Ingredients :

4 quarts of the small field daisy blossoms
1 gallon boiling water
2 lemons
2 oranges
3 lbs. brown sugar
½ lb. raisins
1 oz. yeast

Method :

1. Put the daisies in a bowl and cover with the boiling water. Stand until next day, then squeeze the daisies out.

2. Then boil gently the liquid, sliced lemons, oranges and sugar together for 20 minutes. Allow to cool to lukewarm.

3. Add the chopped raisins and stir the yeast in (it should be first dissolved in a little warm water). Leave to ferment 14 days.

4. Then skim, strain and bottle.

DAMSON PORT

Ingredients :

> 4 lbs. damsons
> 1 gallon boiling water
> 4 lbs. sugar

Method :

1. Pour the boiling water over the damsons and leave them 10 days, stirring and squeezing them each day. Then run through a jelly bag and afterwards strain twice without squeezing. This will save a lot of wine later.

2. Add the sugar to the strained liquid and stir until it is dissolved. Add a teacupful of boiling water to raise the temperature and leave to ferment 14 days.

3. Skim and bottle, corking very loosely.

DAMSON WINE

Ingredients :

> 4 lbs. damsons
> 1 gallon boiling water
> 4 lbs. sugar
> 1 lb. wheat
> 1 oz. yeast ; 1 slice toast

Method :

1. Pour the boiling water over the damsons. Leave to stand 10 days, mashing the fruit daily, then strain, taking care to get all the moisture out of the pulp before you throw it away.

2. Add the wheat and sugar to the liquid and stir until the latter is dissolved. Then spread the yeast on the toast and float in the liquid, leaving 21 days to ferment.

3. Then strain and bottle. Keep 1 year. A rich, heavy body.

DANDELION WINE —

Ingredients :

1 gallon dandelion flower petals
1 gallon boiling water
1 orange
1 lemon
3 lbs. sugar
An inch of whole ginger—well bruised
½ oz. yeast on a slice of toast

Method :

1. Wash the dandelion flowers as they are always gritty, then cover them with the boiling water. Let them stand 3 days, stirring often, before squeezing all the flowers out.

2. Put the liquid into a pan, add the thinly pared yellow rind off the lemon and orange, the sugar and ginger, and the lemon and orange sliced. Boil for 30 minutes. Let cool.

3. Then spread the yeast on toast and float in the liquid. Ferment for 6 days then strain and bottle, corking loosely until all fermentation ceases.

ELDERBERRY GINGER WINE

Ingredients :

1 gallon elderberries
1 gallon water
3½ lbs. sugar
1 oz. whole ginger

Method :

1. Strip the elderberries off the fleshy stems. Add to the water and boil 15 minutes, then strain, throwing the pulp away.

2. Add the sugar, stir until dissolved. Let it ferment 14 days, then skim and bottle.

3. Add the whole ginger well bruised when the wine is 6 months old, then keep 1 month and use.

ELDERBERRY PORT (1)

Ingredients :

> Elderberry juice
> To every quart allow ¾ lb. white sugar and
> ¼ lb. chopped raisins.

Method :

1. Take the elderberries as they turn black to get a full red colour. Strip them from the fleshy stalks and put in a jar.

2. Put the jar in a pan of hot water over heat and draw all the juice from the berries.

3. Strain and measure the juice and put the sugar to it. Stir until it is dissolved, add the chopped raisins and leave to ferment for 3 weeks. Then skim and bottle, corking very loosely. Keep 12 months.

ELDERBERRY PORT (2)

Ingredients :

> 2 quarts of elderberries
> 1 gallon water
> 3 lbs. sugar
> ½ lb. large raisins
> 1 oz. yeast, on a large slice of toast

Method :

1. Strip the berries off the fleshy stalks. Put them with the water and boil for 15 minutes when all the goodness will be in the liquor. Strain, throwing the pulp away.

2. Add the sugar and chopped raisins to the liquid and simmer gently for 20 minutes.

3. Let it cool, then add the yeast spread on the toast, and leave to ferment for 14 days, then skim and bottle.

4. Cork lightly, then after fermentation has ceased, firmly. Keep 12 months.

ELDERBERRY PORT (3)
(Strong and rich)

Ingredients :

1 gallon water
1 gallon elderberries
1 lb. wheat
3½ lbs. sugar
½ lb. large raisins
1 oz. yeast

Method :

1. Strip the berries off the fleshy stalks. Boil with the water for 15 minutes, then strain through a jelly bag, without squeezing. Throw the pulp away.

2. Add the sugar and chopped raisins to the liquid and stir until dissolved.

3. When lukewarm add the wheat and sprinkle yeast over the top. Let it ferment 20 days, then skim, strain and bottle, corking loosely. Keep 12 months.

ELDERBERRY WINE

Ingredients :

1 gallon elderberries
1 gallon water
3 lbs. sugar

Method :

1. Strip the elderberries from the fleshy stems. Add the water and boil together for 15 minutes.

2. Strain and throw the pulp away. Add the sugar to the liquid and let it ferment for 14 days ; then skim and bottle.

3. Keep a year.

ELDERFLOWER WINE (1)

Ingredients :

> 1 pint elder flowers
> 8 pints water
> 3½ lbs. white sugar
> ½ lb. raisins
> 3 sliced lemons
> ½ oz. yeast

Method :

1. Pick the flowers off the thick main stems and put them in a pan with the water and simmer for 15 minutes.

2. Put in a bowl and add sugar, chopped raisins and lemons. Stir until the sugar is dissolved. When lukewarm sprinkle the yeast on top.

3. Leave to ferment 14 days then remove scum and strain very gently into another jar, being careful not to disturb the sendiment. Then bottle. It is like champagne.

ELDERFLOWER WINE (2)

Ingredients :

> 1 gallon elderflower (no fleshy green stems)
> 1 gallon water
> 3 lbs. sugar
> Rind and juice of 3 lemons
> 1 oz. yeast

Method :

1. Boil the water and sugar together for 10 minutes.

2. Put the flowerlets and lemon rind into a bowl, pour over the boiling liquid then add the lemon juice. When lukewarm add the yeast by sprinkling it on top. Leave 4 days then strain.

3. Leave to stand 3 weeks before bottling, corking loosely.

FIG WINE

Ingredients :

> 3 lbs. figs
> ½ lb. raisins
> 3 lbs. apples (sour windfalls)
> 1 gallon water
> 3½ lbs. sugar

Method :

1. Boil the figs in the water until very tender. Remove the figs and use them as food.

2. Chop the apples and raisins up and add to the water with the sugar. Stir often.

3. Leave to ferment 1 month then strain and stand a further 14 days before bottling.

FLOWER WINE

Ingredients :

> 1 quart dandelion blossoms
> 1 quart elder blossom
> 1 quart cowslip petals (no green)
> 1 gallon water
> 4 lbs. sugar
> 1 oz. yeast ; 1 slice toast

Method :

1. Wash the dandelions because they are gritty, then put all the flowers in a bowl.

2. Boil the sugar and water together and pour it over the flowers. Leave 3 days then strain.

3. Add the yeast spread on both sides of the toast and float it in the liquid. Leave to ferment 14 days, then skim and bottle.

GINGER LEMON WINE

Ingredients :

1 oz. lump ginger
4 lemons
3½ lbs. sugar
¼ lb. raisins
1 oz. yeast ; 1 slice toast
1 gallon hot water

Method :

1. Bruise the ginger and cut the lemons up in slices. Chop the raisins and put them in a bowl. Pour the water over.

2. Immediately add the sugar and stir it away, then when lukewarm spread the yeast on toast and float in the bowl.

3. Leave 15 days then skim and bottle.

GINGER WINE (1)

Ingredients :

½ oz. essence ginger
½ oz. capsicum
⅓ oz. tartaric acid
½ oz. burnt sugar
3 lbs. sugar
7 pints boiling water

Method :

1. Take a bottle to the chemist's and he will put the ingredients in, excepting the tartaric acid, which is in a powder.

2. Put the sugar and tartaric acid in a bowl and pour the boiling water over. Let it stand until cold and then add the other ingredients and bottle.

GINGER WINE (2)

Ingredients :

2 drams cayenne
2 teaspoonfuls lemon essence
4 drams essence of ginger
1 oz. burnt sugar
> Take a bottle to the chemist for the above.

¾ oz. tartaric acid
3 lbs. sugar
3 quarts boiling water

Method :

1. Put the sugar in a big bowl, add the contents of bottle from chemist, and boiling water. Stir until the sugar is dissolved. Leave overnight.

2. Add the tartaric acid to the bulk after dissolving it in a little of the wine. Bottle and keep 14 days.

3. This used in equal quantities with soda water makes a fine, sharp teetotal cocktail.

GINGER WINE (3)
(Fermented)

Ingredients :

1½ ozs. ginger (whole)
3 lbs. sugar
2 lemons
2 oranges
1 lb. raisins
½ oz. yeast; a slice of toast
1 gallon water

Method :

1. Bruise the ginger and put it into a pan with the thinly pared yellow rinds of lemons and oranges and sugar. Bring to the boil and simmer for 30 minutes, then strain and allow to cool.

2. Add the chopped raisins, juice of oranges and lemons and the yeast spread on both sides of the toast. Leave to ferment 14 days, then strain and bottle.

GOLDEN DROP GOOSEBERRY WINE
(Garden and Golden Champagne)

Ingredients :

> 1 gallon golden drops
> 1 gallon water
> 4 lbs. sugar
> 1 tablespoonful of raisins

Method :

1. Pull the gooseberries when ripe and dry and place in a bowl. Cover with water, add the chopped raisins and squeeze and mash every day for 14 days.

2. Then squeeze the pulp out, getting every drop of moisture before throwing it away, then strain the liquid.

3. Add the sugar and stir until dissolved, then let it ferment 14 days before skimming and bottling.

4. Keep 9 months to get a body as well as delicious flavour.

GOLDEN GOOSEBERRY WINE

Ingredients :

> 1 gallon yellow gooseberries
> 1 gallon water
> ½ lb. large raisins
> 1 lb. wheat
> 1 oz. yeast
> 4 lbs. sugar

Method :

1. Put the gooseberries, sugar, chopped raisins and wheat in a bowl, cover with warm (not hot) water and sprinkle the yeast on top *when* lukewarm.

2. Squeeze every day for 14 days and stir well up.

3. Then strain and bottle.

To save work in pouring over from the bottles I found it best to replace this wine in a jar after straining. Then, at the end of 14 days, I poured the clear off and bottled it, leaving a good lot of sediment in the bottom of the jar.

GOLDEN PLUM WINE (1)

Ingredients :

1 gallon yellow plums, very ripe
1 gallon cold water
4 lbs. Demerara sugar

Method :

1. Put the plums and water in a bowl and squeeze and stir them every day for 8 days.

2. Then strain out the pulp and squeeze every drop of moisture from it before throwing it away.

3. Strain the liquid and stir the sugar away in it and leave to ferment 14 days, then skim and bottle.

GOLDEN PLUM WINE (2)

(Extra strong)

Ingredients :

1 gallon plums
1 gallon water
1 lb. wheat
1 oz. yeast
4 lbs. Demerara sugar

Method :

1. Put the plums, water, wheat and sugar into a jar and stir until the sugar is dissolved.

2. Then stir the yeast in a little warm water and add.

3. Leave 14 days, stirring every day, then strain and squeeze all the moisture out of the pulp before throwing it away.

4. Strain the liquid twice and bottle it.

GOLDEN WINE

Ingredients :

3 quarts of yellow gooseberries
1 quart white currants
1 gallon warm water
1 lb. raisins
1 lb. wheat
1 oz. yeast
4 lbs. sugar

Method :

1. Put the gooseberries, white currants, sugar, chopped raisins and wheat in a bowl. Cover with warm water and sprinkle the yeast on top.

2. Stir and squeeze every day for 14 days, then strain and squeeze every drop out of the pulp before throwing it away.

3. Strain the liquid twice and bottle it.

Old-fashioned gardens usually have one white currant bush. By adding the fruit in this way a fine, unusual wine is got.

GRAPE PORT

Ingredients :

7 lbs. green grapes
2 lbs. ripe brambles
4 lbs. sugar
1 gallon water
1 pint water

Method :

1. Cover the grapes with the water and squeeze and stir them for 14 days, then strain and throw the pulp away.

2. Add the sugar and stir until it is dissolved. Set in a warm place to ferment.

3. Take the brambles and add the pint of water and simmer for 15 minutes, then strain and when cool add the juice to the grape liquid. Leave 14 days then strain and bottle. Keep a twelve-month.

GRAPE WINE (1)

Ingredients :

> 6 lbs. grapes (any kind)
> 1 gallon of cold water
> 3½ lbs. white sugar

Method :

1. Bruise each grape between the finger and thumb, cover with the cold water. Stir each day and press the grapes for 7 days. Then strain, throwing the pulp away.

2. Strain a second time through a clean tea towel. Add the sugar and stir until it is dissolved, then add a teacupful of boiling water and set the wine in a warm place to ferment.

3. When fermented 14 days skim and bottle, corking lightly until all hissing ceases.

GRAPE WINE (2)

Ingredients :

> 4 lbs. grapes (any kind)
> 12 vine leaves (give a fine, sharp flavour)
> 1 gallon of warm water
> 4 lbs. sugar
> 2 large slices of toast ; 1 oz. yeast

Method :

1. Toast the bread and cut it into squares. Put it with the grapes and grape leaves in a bowl. Add the water and sugar and stir until it is dissolved.

2. On the second day squeeze all the grapes and scatter the yeast on top. Add a teacupful of boiling water and leave to ferment 21 days.

3. Then strain and bottle.

GRAPE WINE (1)
(Northrop)

Ingredients :

> 7 lbs. grapes (unevenly ripened ones in a cold green-
> house was what I used)
> 7 quarts boiling water
> 7 lbs. white sugar

Method :

1. Pour the water over the grapes and leave 1 month, mashing and stirring every day, then strain and throw away the pulp.

2. Add the sugar to the liquid and allow to work for 3 months—then strain and bottle.

3. At 6 months old this was a strong and white wine.

GRAPE WINE (2)
(Stockton)

Ingredients :

> 3 lbs. cheap small black grapes (these are to be had in
> the markets in Summer)
> 4 quarts cold water
> 3 lbs. sugar

Method :

1. Put the grapes in a bowl and crush them. Cover with the cold water. Stand 5 days, stirring several times each day, then strain.

2. Add the sugar, stir until it dissolves and set in a warm place to ferment.

3. Leave 10 days then strain and bottle.

GREENGAGE CHAMPAGNE

Ingredients :

> 4 lbs. greengages
> 20 vine leaves
> 1 gallon water
> 4 lbs. sugar
> 1 slice toast ; 1 oz. yeast

Method :

1. Put the greengages and vine leaves in a bowl, cover with cold water. Take the vine leaves out in 3 days but mash and stir the plums for 8 days, then strain.

2. Then add the sugar and yeast spread on both sides of the toast and leave to ferment 14 days.

3. Skim and bottle.

GREENGAGE WINE

Ingredients :

> 4 lbs. greengages
> 1 gallon water
> 4 lbs. sugar

Method :

1. Pour the water over the greengages, and stand 8 days mashing and stirring daily, then strain.

2. Add the sugar and put in a warm place to ferment for 14 days then strain and bottle.

GREEN GOOSEBERRY CHAMPAGNE

Ingredients :

1 gallon gooseberries
12 grape leaves
1 gallon cold water
4 lbs. white sugar

Method :

1. Pull the green gooseberries when they are large and juicy—but remember they must be bone dry. Put the gooseberries into a bowl with the vine leaves down amongst them. Cover with water. Mash the fruit and stir occasionally. Leave 12 days and then squeeze every drop of moisture from the gooseberries and leaves before throwing them away.

2. Strain the liquid and add the sugar. Stir until it is dissolved and put in a warm room to ferment.

3. Leave 8 days, then skim and bottle.

GREEN WINE

Ingredients :

A good big bouquet of balm (stalks and leaves are used)
1 gallon water
3 lbs. sugar
1 lb. raisins
1 oz. yeast ;   1 large slice toast

Method :

1. Boil the water and pour it over the balm. Leave 3 days then take the balm out, pressing all the moisture out.

2. Add the sugar, diced toast and chopped raisins to the liquid and sprinkle the yeast on top. Ferment 14 days then skim, strain and bottle. Delicious.

HEATHER WINE

Ingredients :

> Heather, when it is in full bloom
> Water—to 1 gallon 4 lbs. sugar
> 2 lemons
> 2 oranges
> 1 oz. yeast ; a large slice of toast

Method :

1. Cut the heather when in full bloom and cover it with water and boil for 1 hour, then strain the liquid off and measure. Leave until lukewarm.

2. Slice the oranges and lemons into the liquid, add the sugar and stir until it is dissolved. Spread the yeast on both sides of toast and float it in the liquid. Leave 14 days to ferment then skim and strain and bottle. Keep 6 months.

HEDGEROW AMBER

Ingredients :

> 1 gallon of hips
> 1 gallon of cold water
> 3½ lbs. sugar
> 1 oz. yeast ; 1 slice toast
> 3 lemons
> 3 oranges
> ½ lb. raisins

Method :

1. Pick the hips when they are red and put them into a bowl. Add the water and mash the hips with a wooden spoon, or your hand.

2. Leave for a week, stirring each day, then strain through muslin and throw the pulp away.

3. Add the sugar to the liquid and stir until dissolved. Add the sliced lemons, oranges and chopped raisins. Spread the yeast on toast and float on top and leave for 16 days.

4. Strain and bottle and keep for 6 months.

HEDGEROW PORT

Ingredients :

> 3 lbs. ripe brambles
> 2 lbs. ripe bullace plums or damsons
> 1 gallon water
> 1 lb. wheat
> ½ lb. large raisins
> ½ oz. yeast
> 4 lbs. sugar

Method :

1. Pour the boiling water over the damsons and brambles and let them stand five days. Squeeze and stir every day.

2. Strain and squeeze every drop of moisture from the fruit before throwing it away.

3. Then strain the liquid through 3 thicknesses of muslin.

4. Add the sugar, wheat and raisins, stir until the sugar is dissolved, then add one breakfast cupful of boiling water, and sprinkle the yeast over the top.

5. Let it ferment a month, skimming the top off once a week, then strain and bottle.

HIP WINE

Ingredients :

> 1 gallon hips
> 1 gallon cold water
> 3½ lbs. sugar
> 1 oz. yeast ; 1 slice toast

Method :

1. Pick the hips when they are red and put them into a bowl. Add the water and mash the hips with a wooden spoon or your hand.

2. Leave for a week, stirring each day, then strain through muslin and throw the pulp away.

3. Add the sugar to the liquid and stir well until it is dissolved. Then spread the yeast on the toast and leave for 14 days.

4. Strain and bottle and keep for 6 months.

HOCK

Ingredients :

6 potatoes, the size of an egg
3 oranges
3 lemons
1 lb. large raisins
3½ lbs. Demerara sugar
1 gallon boiling water

Method :

1. Cut the potatoes up small, slice the oranges and lemons, add the chopped raisins and sugar.

2. Pour over the boiling water and stir until the sugar is dissolved.

3. Cover and stand 16 days then strain and bottle.

HONEY WINE

Ingredients :

½ oz. hops
3½ lbs. honey
1 lb. wheat
1 oz. yeast
½ lb. whole raisins
1 gallon water

Method :

1. Boil the hops in the water for 20 minutes and then strain and make the liquid up to 1 gallon.

2. When lukewarm add the wheat, chopped raisins and honey. Stir until it is dissolved then stir in the yeast after it has been dissolved in a little water.

3. Leave 16 days to ferment then skim and bottle.

HOP WINE

Ingredients :

1 oz. hops
1 oz. white whole ginger
1 orange
1 lemon
3 lbs. sugar
1 gallon water
1 oz. yeast
½ lb. large raisins
1 slice of toast

Method :

1. Pour the boiling water on to the hops, leave overnight then strain.

2. Into the liquid put the sliced lemon and orange, sugar, bruised ginger and chopped raisins. Stir until the sugar is dissolved.

3. Spread the yeast on both sides of the toast and float on the liquid. Leave to ferment 3 weeks.

4. Then skim and bottle.

KITCHEN WINE

Ingredients :

3 grape fruits
3 lemons
3 oranges
1 lb. raisins
1 oz. yeast ; 1 large slice toast
3½ lbs. sugar
1 gallon cold water

Method :

1. Peel the fruit as whole as possible and throw the peel in the water (on no account squeeze it or the wine will be bitter).

2. Cut the fruit up into dice and add to the liquid with the chopped raisins and sugar and stir until the sugar dissolves. Then spread the yeast on the toast and float it on the top. Leave 16 days to ferment, then having squeezed well all the pulp (but the skins) strain.

3. Stand 1 week before bottling.

LEMON WINE

Ingredients :

> 12 big juicy lemons
> 1 gallon boiling water
> 4 lbs. sugar
> 1 slice toast ; 1 oz. yeast
> 1 lb. raisins

Method :

1. Cut the lemons in half and squeeze all the juice from them. (Put it aside in a basin.)

2. Put the skins in a bowl and pour the water over. Stand 4 days then strain.

3. Add the sugar and lemon juice to the liquid and stir until sugar is dissolved, then add the chopped raisins and yeast spread on both sides of the toast. Leave to ferment 14 days, then strain.

4. Stand the wine 10 days before bottling.

LIME WINE (1)

Pull the sweetly scented lime blossoms when the flower is open full, from the lime trees and dry them in the sun.

Ingredients :

> 1 pint of lime blossoms
> 1 gallon water
> 3½ lbs. white sugar
> ½ lb. large raisins
> 1 large slice of toast
> 1 oz. yeast

Method :

1. Put the flowers into the pan with the water and simmer for 15 minutes then turn in a big bowl.

2. Add the sugar, chopped raisins and toast with the yeast spread on both sides. Leave 14 days.

3. Then strain and stand the liquid in the jar one week, then strain off the clear liquid and bottle.

LIME WINE (2)
(Very Strong)

Ingredients :

½ gallon lime flowers
1 gallon water
1 lb. wheat
1 oz. yeast
1 lb. raisins
3¾ lbs. sugar

Method :

1. Boil the lime flowers in the water for 30 minutes then strain and leave the liquid to cool to lukewarm.

2. Then add the sugar, wheat and chopped raisins to the liquid.

3. Dissolve the yeast and stir it in and let all stand for 21 days to ferment.

4. Then strain and bottle.

Point to remember : The lime blossoms must be dried in the sun to bring up the flavour.

MANGOLD-WURZEL WINE
(Make in March)

Ingredients :

1 gallon mangolds
1 gallon water
3 lbs. sugar
1 oz. yeast
½ oz. of hops

Method :

1. Clean the mangolds by washing well and take off the roughest roots. Cut into dice and boil in the water one hour, then strain.

2. Put the sugar in the liquid and stir until dissolved. Put the hops in and when lukewarm sprinkle the yeast on top, and leave 3 weeks to ferment.

3. Then strain and bottle.

MARIGOLD WINE (1)

Ingredients :

    1 quart marigold flowers
    1 gallon water
    3½ lbs. sugar
    1 lb. wheat
    1 oz. yeast

Method :

1. Put the water and flowers into a big bowl, stir daily for 8 days then strain and throw the pulp away.

2. Add the sugar and wheat and stir until the sugar is dissolved. Sprinkle the yeast on top and let it ferment 21 days.

3. Then skim and bottle.

4. Use all the flower head but no green stalk as it is harsh and bitter.

MARIGOLD WINE (2)

Ingredients :

    1 quart marigold flowers
    1½ gallons cold water
    2½ lbs. sugar
    ½ lb. honey
    1 oz. yeast ; 1 large slice toast
    2 lemons
    1 lb. raisins

Method :

1. Gather the flowers on a dry day, cover with water and allow to stand 8 days. Then strain and throw all the pulp away.

2. Add the sliced lemons, chopped raisins, sugar and honey to the liquid. Spread the yeast on toast and float on top and leave to ferment 21 days.

3. Then skim and bottle.

MARROW WINE

Ingredients :

> 5 lbs. marrow (leave the seeds in)
> 3 lbs. sugar
> 2 lemons
> 2 oranges
> 1 oz. ginger
> 1 gallon water

Method :

1. Grate the marrow, slice the fruit and bruise the ginger well. Pour over the boiling water and stand 10 days, stirring frequently, then strain.

2. Add the sugar to the liquid and let it ferment 7 days then skim and bottle.

Good at the end of 6 months, and is an excellent way to make up the marrow pulp when jam making.

MAYFLOWER WINE (1)
(Hawthorn)

Ingredients :

> ½ gallon May blossom
> 1 gallon water
> 3 lbs. sugar
> 1 lb. wheat
> ½ lb. raisins
> 1 oz. yeast
> 1 slice of toast

Method :

1. Put the May blossom in a bowl.

2. Boil the sugar and water together and pour over the May blossom. Let it stand to cool.

3. When lukewarm add the chopped raisins, wheat and spread the yeast on toast and put among the liquid.

4. Leave to ferment 16 days, stirring every day ; then strain and bottle.

MAYFLOWER WINE (2) (Double Strength)
(Hawthorn)

Ingredients :

> 1 gallon water
> 1 gallon Hawthorn flowers
> 3 lbs. sugar
> 1 oz. lump ginger
> 2 oranges
> 1 lemon
> 1 oz. yeast ; a large slice of toast
> 1 lb. large raisins

Method :

1. Into a bowl put the flowers, lump ginger well bruised, and sliced oranges and lemons and chopped raisins.

2. Boil the water and sugar together and pour over all in the bowl.

3. When lukewarm spread the yeast on the toast and float in the liquid. Leave to ferment 16 days, then strain and bottle.

MULBERRY WINE

Ingredients :

> ½ gallon mulberries
> 1 gallon water
> 3½ lbs. white sugar
> 1 oz. yeast ; 1 slice toast

Method :

1. Put the mulberries in the water and boil for half an hour, then strain.

2. Add the sugar and stir until it is dissolved then leave until luke-warm.

3. Spread the yeast on toast, float it in the liquid and leave to ferment 14 days then skim and bottle.

OAK LEAF WINE

Ingredients :

2 gallons oak leaves
1 gallon boiling water
4 lbs. sugar
½ oz. whole ginger (well bruised)
1 oz. yeast ; 1 slice toast

Method :

1. Pick the oak leaves in October when they are withered, put in a bowl and pour the boiling water over. Leave standing 3 or 4 days then strain and throw the leaves away.

2. Add the sugar and ginger to the liquid and boil for 20 minutes.

3. When lukewarm add the yeast on the toast and ferment for 10 days, then skim and bottle.

ORANGE WINE (1)

Ingredients :

1 gallon water
3 lbs. sugar
5 Jaffa oranges
1 Seville orange
1 lemon
1 lb. wheat
¼ lb. raisins
1 oz. yeast

Method :

1. Strain the juice from the fruit and put the skins (thinly pared yellow only) into the water and bring to the boil, and boil for 15 minutes. Then strain the peel out of the liquid.

2. Add the sugar, juice, chopped raisins and wheat. Add the yeast (creamed with a little water) when the liquid is lukewarm.

3. Let it ferment 21 days, then strain and bottle.

ORANGE WINE (2)

Ingredients :

    24 oranges (no rind)
    3½ lbs. sugar
    1 gallon cold water
    ¼ lb. large raisins

Method :

1. Peel the oranges but do not use the peel.
2. Cut the fruit in slices and cover with cold water. Squeeze and stir daily for 10 days, then strain and throw away the pulp.
3. Add the sugar and chopped raisins to the liquid and stir until it is dissolved, then set in a warm place to ferment for 14 days.
4. Then strain and bottle.

ORANGE WINE (3)
(Hovingham)

Ingredients :

    30 oranges
    2 lemons
    1 gallon cold water
    3½ lbs. sugar

Method :

1. Squeeze out the juice of the fruit into a basin.
2. Place the skins after squeezing into a bowl with the water and let them stand for 4 days, stirring daily, then strain.
3. Add the sugar to the liquid and stir until it is dissolved. Add all the juice and put in a warm place to ferment for 14 days, then skim and allow to stand 6 weeks before bottling.

ORANGE WINE (4)
(Spennymoor)

Ingredients :

> 12 oranges
> 4 lbs. loaf sugar
> 1 lb. large raisins
> 1 gallon water

Method :

1. Peel 6 oranges and put the skins in the oven to brown. When well browned pour over them 1 quart of boiling water.

2. Cut up the remaining oranges and put over them 3 quarts cold water. When the brown liquid is cold mix it in also. Add the chopped raisins and stir daily for 8 days, then strain.

3. Add the sugar and allow to ferment for 8 more days, then strain and bottle.

ORCHARD WINE

Ingredients :

> 4 lbs. apples
> 4 lbs. pears
> 1 gallon water
> 3½ lbs. sugar
> ½ lb. raisins

Method :

1. Cut up the apples and pears—all the little, un-evenly ripened will do—and cover them with the water.

2. Add the sugar and chopped raisins and let all stand 30 days, squeezing and stirring daily. Then strain.

3. Stand the liquor a further 15 days before bottling. Cork loosely.

PARSNIP SHERRY —

Ingredients :

>4 lbs. parsnips
>½ oz. hops
>½ lb. malt
>1 gallon water
>4 lbs. Demerara sugar
>1 oz. yeast ; a large slice toast

Method :

1. Clean the parsnips but do not peel them (weigh after cleaning). Cut into slices and boil gently in half the water until parsnips are tender, then strain.

2. Put the hops in the remaining water and boil until all the goodness is extracted. Strain and add the liquids together.

3. Stir in it ½ lb. malt and all the sugar. Spread the yeast on toast and add to the bowl when lukewarm.

4. Let it ferment 14 days then skim and bottle, corking loosely.

PARSNIP WINE

Ingredients :

>4 lbs. parsnips
>1 gallon water
>3½ lbs. sugar
>1 oz. lump ginger
>½ lb. wheat
>1 lemon
>½ lb. large raisins
>1 oz. yeast on a slice of toast

Method :

1. Clean the parsnips (weigh after paring), cut them into two and put them into the water and boil gently until they are tender ; strain.

2. Add the sugar and lump ginger (well bruised) to the liquid and boil for 5 minutes.

3. Turn the liquid into a bowl, add the juice and rind of the lemon and the chopped raisins. Let it cool before adding the yeast spread on toast, and the wheat.

4. Ferment 14 days then skim and bottle.

PEA POD WINE

Ingredients :

    2 gallons pea pods
    1 gallon water
    4 lbs. sugar
    $\frac{1}{2}$ oz. yeast
    1 slice toast

Method :

1. Boil the pods in the water until tender and they have turned yellow, then strain.

2. Add the sugar to the liquid and the creamed yeast on toast and leave to ferment for 21 days, then skim and bottle.

3. At first this wine is cloudy but clears itself, and is delicious at 6 months old.

PEAR WINE

Ingredients :

    4 lbs. pears
    1 lb. raisins
    $3\frac{1}{2}$ lbs. sugar
    1 gallon water
    1 cake of shredded wheat

Method :

1. Cut the pears up and cover them with water. Add the raisins, sugar and shredded wheat, broken up. Leave 21 days, stirring and breaking up the fruit and raisins every day, then strain.

2. Leave the liquid in the jar to stand 14 days before bottling—when you take the clear off the top.

A PORT-LIKE BREW

Ingredients :

½ gallon of rhubarb, cut up small
½ gallon of cold water
½ gallon of brambles
½ gallon of water
4 lbs. of sugar

Method :

1. Cut the rhubarb small and cover with cold water. Let it stand 14 days.

2. Then strain and add half the sugar to the liquid and allow to stand one week fermenting before putting into bottles or a grey hen.

3. A month later, or when the brambles are ripe, cover ½ gallon of brambles with ½ gallon of boiling water.

4. Let it stand 8 days then squeeze and strain.

5. Add the remaining 2 lbs. of sugar to this bramble juice and allow to ferment 1 week, then strain into the rhubarb liquor and keep until midsummer—simply gorgeous.

POTATO WINE (1)

Ingredients :

1 lb. wheat
1 lb. large raisins
1 lb. potatoes
4 lbs. sugar
1 gallon water
1 oz. yeast

Method :

1. Put wheat, chopped raisins and potatoes in a bowl (peel the potatoes and cut them up very small). Add the sugar, cover with the water.

2. Add the yeast dissolved in a little warm water. Stir well and leave to ferment for 3 weeks, then strain and bottle.

3. This is a fine golden wine.

POTATO WINE (2)

Ingredients :

> 5 lbs. potatoes (do not peel them)
> 1 gallon water
> 2 lemons
> 2 oranges
> 1 oz. whole ginger—well bruised
> 4 lbs. Demerara sugar

Method :

1. Put the potatoes with the water, bring to the boil and boil for 10 minutes, then strain out the potatoes.

2. Add to the liquid the rinds of lemons and oranges, add the ginger and boil for a further 15 minutes.

3. Have ready a bowl containing the sliced oranges, lemons and sugar. Strain the liquid over and let it stand for 48 hours, then bottle and cork loosely. Keep 6 months.

4. This is a fine golden wine.

PRIMROSE WINE (1)

Ingredients ·

> 4 quarts primrose petals
> 1 gallon boiling water
> 2 oranges
> 2 lemons
> 3½ lbs. sugar

Method :

1. Pour the boiling water over the flowers and sliced fruit. Let it stand 5 days stirring and squeezing the fruit every day, then strain.

2. Add the sugar and stir until it is dissolved then stand 14 days to ferment before skimming, straining and bottling.

PRIMROSE WINE (2)

Ingredients :

2 quarts primrose petals
1 gallon cold water
1 lb. raisins
3 lbs. sugar
1 lb. wheat
1 oz. yeast

Method :

1. Put the primroses into the water and leave 8 days, then squeeze them out.

2. Put the chopped raisins, sugar and wheat into the liquid and stir until the sugar is dissolved, then sprinkle the yeast on top and leave to ferment 28 days.

3. Skim, strain and bottle.

PRUNE CHAMPAGNE

Ingredients :

2 lbs. prunes
3 lbs. rhubarb
1 gallon cold water
4 lbs. sugar

Method :

1. Put the prunes and rhubarb—the latter cut small —into a bowl and cover with the cold water. Let it stand 14 days, mashing the fruit and stirring it up every day, then strain.

2. Add the sugar and leave to ferment for 14 days, then strain and bottle but do not cork closely until fermentation ceases.

PRUNE SHERRY ——

Ingredients :

2 lbs. prunes
1 gallon water
½ lb. raisins
4 lbs. sugar
1 large slice toast ; 1 oz. yeast

Method :

1. Cover the prunes with cold water and let them stand 14 days, stirring and mashing the fruit, then strain being careful to extract all moisture from the fruit before throwing the pulp away.

2. Add the sugar, chopped raisins and the yeast spread on both sides of the toast. Leave to ferment 21 days then skim and bottle, corking loosely.

QUINCE WINE

Ingredients :

2 dozen quinces
1 gallon water
3 lbs. sugar
½ lb. raisins
2 lemons
1 oz. yeast ; 1 slice of toast

Method :

1. Peel the quinces thinly and grate up the flesh. Put it in the water and boil for 30 minutes, then strain and throw the pulp away.

2. Slice the lemons into the liquid, add the sugar and chopped raisins and when lukewarm spread the yeast on both sides of the toast and float it in the liquid. Leave to ferment 16 days, then strain.

3. Leave the liquid to stand a week before bottling and keep a twelve month.

RAISIN WINE —

Ingredients :

                1 oz. tea
                1 gallon water
                2 lbs. large raisins
                1 lb. wheat
                1 oz. yeast
                4 lemons
                3½ lbs. sugar

Method :

1. Tie the tea loosely in a muslin bag and pour over the boiling water and let it mash. Lift the bag out when the liquid is lukewarm.

2. To the liquid add the chopped raisins, sugar, wheat and sliced lemons.

3. Dissolve the yeast in a little of the liquid and stir it in.

4. Leave to ferment 21 days, stirring often, then strain and bottle.

RED CURRANT WINE

Ingredients :

                1 gallon red currants
                1 gallon boiling water
                4 lbs. sugar

Method :

1. Pour the boiling water over the red currants and let them stand 4 or 5 days, squeezing and stirring every day, then strain taking care to get all the juice from the pulp before throwing it away.

2. Add the sugar to the liquid and stir it away. Set aside to ferment for 14 days then skim, strain and bottle and keep 2 years.

RED MEAD

Ingredients :

> 1 gallon water
> 4½ lbs. honey
> 3 quarts red currant juice
> 1 lb. raisins
> 1 oz. yeast
> 1 slice toast

Method :

1. Boil the honey and water together.

2. When cool add the red currant juice, chopped raisins and yeast spread on the toast. Allow to ferment 16 days.

3. Then skim and strain and stand 10 days before bottling.

RED PORT

Ingredients :

> 3 quarts red brambles (blackberries)
> 1 quart black ones
> 1 gallon water
> 4 lbs. sugar
> ½ lb. wheat
> ½ lb. large raisins
> ½ oz. yeast

Method :

1. Put the brambles and water into the pan. Bring to the boil and simmer gently for 10 minutes or until all the goodness is in the water.

2. Strain and squeeze every drop of moisture from the fruit before throwing it away.

3. Run the liquid through three thicknesses of muslin.

4. Put in the sugar and stir it away. When lukewarm add the wheat and chopped raisins, and sprinkle the yeast over the top.

5. Stand for 3 weeks, skimming the top now and again, then bottle. Keep 8 months.

RED RASPBERRY WINE

Ingredients :

> 1 gallon raspberries
> 1 gallon water
> 4 lbs. sugar

Method :

1. Cover the fruit with the boiling water and leave 7 days, stirring and mashing the fruit every day. Then strain, getting all the moisture from the pulp before throwing it away.

2. Add the sugar and stir until it is dissolved then leave to ferment 14 days. Skim and strain.

3. Bottle and keep 2 years.

RED WINE

Ingredients :

> 1 gallon red brambles (blackberries)
> 1 gallon water
> 1 lb. wheat
> 1 oz. yeast
> 4 lbs. sugar

Method :

1. Boil the brambles in the water until every drop of flavour is extracted from them, then strain.

2. To the liquid add the sugar and stir until it is dissolved. When it becomes lukewarm put in the wheat and sprinkle the yeast over the top.

3. Let it ferment 15 days then skim and bottle.

This is a fine red wine if the brambles are gotten just on the point of turning into black.

RHUBARB AMBER
(Thin)

(Make in June, July or August)

Ingredients :

6 lbs. rhubarb ; 1 gallon cold water
4 lbs. best Demerara sugar
A good pinch of isinglass
2 lbs. ripe brambles ; 1 pint water

Method :

1. Cut the rhubarb up small, put in a bowl and cover with the water. Leave 14 days, stirring and squeezing each day.

2. On the 15th day strain and squeeze every drop of moisture from the rhubarb before throwing it away.

3. Add the sugar to the liquor, stir it away and let it ferment for 8 days. Skim and then bottle.

4. In September or October when the brambles are ripe, take 2 lbs. and put in a pan with 1 pint of water, bring to the boil, mash and simmer for 10 minutes. Then strain through a cloth, squeezing every drop of juice from the brambles. Then strain again through a clean tea towel.

5. Turn out the rhubarb wine into a bowl and add the bramble juice. It will need to be well stirred to blend up the two liquids. Bottle and leave for 8 months when it will be ready for use. It requires no more sugar at this stage, and comes up a rich dark amber colour.

RHUBARB-BEETROOT PORT ⟋

Ingredients :

3 lbs. rhubarb
3 lbs. beetroot
1 gallon water
3½ lbs. sugar
1 oz. ginger
½ lb. sultanas
1 oz. yeast
1 lb. wheat

Method :

1. Cut the rhubarb up and put ½ gallon water over it and let it stand 14 days, stirring and squeezing every day, then squeeze the pulp out.

2. Wash the beetroot and boil it in ½ gallon water then when tender use the beet as food and strain the water into the rhubarb liquid.

3. Add the ginger well bruised, the sultanas and wheat and sprinkle the yeast on top and leave 21 days to ferment.

4. Then skim and bottle.

RHUBARB-BLACKCURRANT WINE

Ingredients :

1 gallon rhubarb
1 gallon cold water
4¼ lbs. sugar
3 lbs. ripe blackcurrants
1 pint water

Method :

1. Cut the rhubarb up small and cover with cold water. Stir often and leave 14 days, then strain the pulp out of the liquid, getting all the juice.

2. Add the sugar and stir it away in the liquid and leave it to ferment 1 week, then add to it the blackcurrant juice.

3. This is got by simmering the blackcurrants in 1 pint of water until the goodness is extracted, then strain and add the liquid to the rhubarb brew. Keep 8 months.

4. Loosen the corks now and again and save an explosion.

RHUBARB-CARROT WINE

Ingredients :

>6 lbs. rhubarb
>4 lbs. brown sugar
>1 gallon water
>4 lbs. carrots
>1 lemon

Method :

1. Boil the carrots in the water until tender and use the carrots for food, then strain the hot liquid.

2. Cut up the rhubarb small and slice the lemon. Pour the hot liquid over and stir and squeeze each day for 14 days.

3. Then squeeze out all the rhubarb and strain the liquid.

4. Add the sugar and stir it away and leave to ferment 1 week, then skim and bottle.

5. This is a fine rhubarb wine, well loaded with the mineral salts from the carrots.

RHUBARB CHAMPAGNE (1)

Ingredients :

>1 gallon rhubarb
>1 gallon cold water
>20 vine leaves with stems
>4 lbs. white sugar

Method :

1. Cut up the rhubarb very small and mix the vine leaves with it. Add the sugar and the water ; stir until the sugar is dissolved.

2. Let it ferment 14 days then strain and bottle, *corking* lightly.

RHUBARB CHAMPAGNE (2)

Ingredients :

1 gallon rhubarb
1 gallon cold water
4 lbs. sugar
½ lb. raisins
4 lemons
½ oz. yeast
A good pinch isinglass
1 tablespoonful cracked maize
    (This you buy at the poultry shop)
1 slice of toast

Method :

1. Boil the maize for ¼ hour in 1 quart of the water, then strain and add it to the bulk, making 1 gallon in all.

2. Cut up the rhubarb and place it in a bowl. Cover with the water, leave 14 days, then strain, and throw the pulp away.

3. Add the sugar, chopped raisins and juice and rind of lemons. Stir until sugar is dissolved, then spread yeast over the toast and lay on the wine.

4. Ferment and skim until no more scum rises and put in bottles. It will be very fresh so cork very, very lightly or you will have an explosion.

RHUBARB-COWSLIP WINE

Ingredients :

6 lbs. rhubarb
1 pint cowslip yellow pips
1 gallon cold water
4 lbs. sugar

Method :

1. Put the rhubarb (cut up small) with the yellow flowerettes into the water and stand to mash 14 days, stirring often. Then strain and throw all the pulp away.

2. Add the sugar to the liquid and stir until dissolved.
Leave to ferment 14 days then skim and bottle, corking lightly. Keep 6 months.

RHUBARB-DAMSON PORT —

Ingredients :

>6 lbs. rhubarb
>1 gallon cold water
>4½ lbs. best Demerara sugar
>1 lemon
>2 lbs. damsons
>1 quart boiling water

Method :

1. Cut up the rhubarb small and cover with the cold water. Stir often and let it stand 14 days, then squeeze all the rhubarb out and throw it away. Strain the liquid.

2. Add sugar to liquid (stir it away), juice of the lemon and rind. Let it ferment 1 week ; strain, bottle.

3. Later when damsons are ripe, cover 2 lbs. with the boiling water, squeeze and stir every day. Stand 1 week ; strain, add juice to the rhubarb wine, keep to mature.

Point to remember : The two must be well blended together, and to do this it is best to turn all the wine into a bowl and stir together fully 10 minutes before rebottling.

RHUBARB-DANDELION WINE

Ingredients :

>1 quart dandelion flower heads
>1 gallon water
>1 oz. yeast
>6 lbs. rhubarb
>1 large slice of toast
>4 lbs. sugar

Method :

1. Wash the dandelion flowers in cold water—they are generally very gritty. Then pour the gallon of boiling water over them and leave 24 hours. Squeeze the dandelions out and cut up the rhubarb and put it into the liquid. Leave it 14 days, stirring often, then strain and throw the pulp away.

2. Add the sugar to the liquid and stir until dissolved. Spread the yeast on the toast, and float on top of the wine. Leave to ferment 14 days.

3. Skim and bottle, corking lightly.

RHUBARB-FIG WINE

Ingredients :

6 lbs. rhubarb
1 lb. figs
1 gallon cold water
½ lb. wheat
3¾ lbs. sugar
1 oz. yeast

Method :

1. Put the figs into a gallon of water and simmer until the figs are swollen and juicy and very tender.

2. Strain the water into a big bowl and use the figs as food. This water must be made up to a measured gallon.

3. Cut up the rhubarb small and place in the fig liquid when it is cold. Add the wheat and stand 2 weeks, stirring often. Then strain and throw the pulp away.

4. Add the sugar to the liquid. Stir until it is dissolved, then sprinkle the yeast on top and leave it to ferment 14 days.

5. Then skim and bottle, corking lightly until the fermentation ceases.

RHUBARB GOLDEN CLARET

Ingredients :

6 lbs. rhubarb
1 gallon cold water
4 lbs. best Demerara sugar
1 lemon
3 lbs. sloes
¼ lb. dark barley sugar

Method :

1. Cut up the rhubarb and cover it with the cold water. Stir often and let it stand 14 days, then strain.

2. Add sugar, stir till dissolved. Add juice of lemon and rind. Let it ferment a week then skim and bottle.

3. Later when the sloes are ripe, pour out the wine and add the sloes, breaking them up with the hand. Add the barley sugar and set in a warm place. Leave 14 days, then strain and squeeze the sloes well. Re-bottle and cork lightly. Keep 12 months.

RHUBARB-LOGANBERRY RED WINE

Ingredients :

    1 gallon of rhubarb
    1 gallon of cold water
    1 lemon ; ½ lb. raisins
    5 lbs. white sugar
    Loganberry juice to make a rich red, or
    3 lbs. loganberries ; 1½ pints of water

Method :

1. Cut up the rhubarb small and cover with cold water. Let it stand 14 days then strain and squeeze every drop of juice from the pulp before throwing it away.

2. Add the sugar, chopped raisins and juice and rind of the lemon ; stir until the sugar is dissolved. Let it ferment 7 days, then skim and bottle. Put 3 lbs. loganberries into 1½ pints of water and simmer until all the goodness is extracted (about 30 minutes). Strain and add to the rhubarb liquid. Keep 8 months.

3. Point to remember : Take the loganberries just when they reach the luscious dark red stage.

RHUBARB-MANGEL-WURZEL WINE

Ingredients :

    4 lbs. mangel-wurzels
    1 gallon water
    6 lbs. rhubarb
    3½ lbs. sugar
    1 lb. large raisins

Method :

1. Cut the mangolds up after well washing and put in the water and boil for 1 hour, then strain and let it cool.

2 Cut the rhubarb up small and pour the liquid over. Leave to stand 14 days, squeezing and stirring the liquid daily, then squeeze the pulp out and throw it away.

3. Put the sugar and chopped raisins in the liquid and stir until the sugar is dissolved, then leave to ferment for 1 week.

4. Then skim and bottle.

RHUBARB-ORANGE WINE

Ingredients :

> 1 gallon rhubarb
> 1 gallon cold water
> 6 Jaffa oranges
> 4 lbs. sugar

Method :

1. Cut up the rhubarb very small, peel the yellow rind from the oranges, pour over the cold water, stir often and leave 14 days. Then strain all the pulp out.

2. Add the sugar and orange juice, stir until the sugar is dissolved and ferment for a week. Then strain and bottle, corking lightly until all fermentation ceases.

3. Point to remember : The orange rind must not be squeezed or the wine will be bitter.

RHUBARB-PLUM SHERRY

Ingredients :

> 1 gallon rhubarb
> 1 gallon plums (any sort will do)
> 1½ gallons boiling water
> 6 lbs. sugar

Method :

1. Cut up the rhubarb. Add the plums and water and let all mash 14 days, stirring and squeezing the plums often.

2. Strain the pulp out and add the sugar to the liquid and stir until it is dissolved. Let it ferment 14 days then skim and bottle, corking lightly until fermentation ceases.

RHUBARB PORT

(Extra good)

Ingredients :

> 1 gallon of rhubarb
> 1 gallon cold water
> ½ lb. large raisins
> 4 lbs. sugar
> 6 lemons
> 1 oz. yeast
> 1 slice of toast
> Bramble juice to make it a rich red

Method :

1. Cut up the rhubarb small and cover with cold water. Add the lemon juice and chopped raisins.

2. Let it stand 12 days, stirring every day, then strain and throw away the pulp. Add the sugar to the liquid and stir until it is dissolved. Spread the yeast on a slice of toast and float it on top. Let it ferment 12 days. Skim and bottle.

3. Later when the brambles are ripe add sufficient bramble juice to make the wine a deep rich red, then cork up and keep until Midsummer.

4. It is quite good without the bramble juice, and I often only treat half of this to the bramble juice.

5. Put the brambles in a jar, set them in a pan of hot water until the juice flows freely. The heavy port-like "body" is according to the quantity of pure juice added, but 1 quart is enough.

RHUBARB RED WINE (1)

Ingredients :

6 lbs. rhubarb
1 gallon cold water
4 lbs. white sugar
A good pinch of isinglass
1 quart raspberry juice
½ lb. sugar

Method :

1. Cut up the rhubarb small and cover with cold water. Let it stand 14 days, stirring often, then squeeze all the moisture out of the pulp before throwing it away. Strain this liquid.

2. Add the sugar and isinglass and allow to ferment 1 week, then strain and bottle.

3. When the raspberries ripen put them in a bowl and sprinkle with the ½ lb. sugar and leave overnight. Strain off the juice, measure, and add to the above.

4. You must have 1 quart of pure raspberry juice and use no more than ½ lb. sugar to extract it. The quantity of raspberries needed to produce the juice varies according to the season.

Point to remember : Keep a year to get it at its best.

RHUBARB RED WINE (2)

Ingredients :

½ gallon rhubarb
½ gallon very ripe red gooseberries
4 lbs. sugar
1 gallon of cold water

Method :

1. Cut up rhubarb, cover with half a gallon of cold water. Let it stand 14 days then squeeze out the pulp.

2. Bring the remaining cold water to the boil and put into it the red gooseberries and gently simmer until the goodness is out of the berries. Strain and throw the pulp away. Add the liquids together, put the sugar in, stir it away, then allow to ferment for 14 days.

3. Skim, bottle, cork lightly. Leave a year to mature.

RHUBARB-ROSE WINE

Ingredients :

> 6 lbs. rhubarb
> 1 gallon water
> 2 quarts red rose petals
> 4 lbs. sugar

Method :

1. Boil the water and pour it over the rose petals. Leave overnight then strain through a muslin, throwing the pulp away. Cut up the rhubarb small and put it in the liquid, leave for 14 days, stirring often. Then strain and throw the rhubarb pulp away.

2. Add the sugar to the liquid and stir until dissolved. Allow to ferment 10 days, then skim and bottle, corking lightly.

RHUBARB SHERRY
(Make in August, September or October)

Ingredients :

> 1 gallon cold water
> 6 lbs. rhubarb
> 1 lemon
> 4 lbs. best Demerara sugar
> 6 large raisins
> Isinglass

Method :

1. Cut up the rhubarb very small, put in a crock and cover with cold water. Let it stand a fortnight, stirring and bruising the rhubarb every day.

2. Strain through a colander, squeezing the rhubarb to get all the juice out, and throw the rhubarb away.

3. Then strain the liquor through a clean tea towel.

4. Warm the sugar very slightly (this is to raise the temperature so that fermentation will set up) and add to the liquid. Stir until it is dissolved. Cut the lemon in two, squeeze the juice in and add the squeezed halves. Pull the raisins apart and put them in. Add a big pinch of dry isinglass and stir it in, then leave to ferment for 8 days.

5. Skim and bottle. Leave 8 months to mature.

RHUBARB-STRAWBERRY WINE

Ingredients :

6 lbs. rhubarb
1 gallon water
½ gallon ripe strawberries
4 lbs. sugar

Method :

1. Cut up the rhubarb small, cover with half the water.

2. Bring the strawberries to the boil in the other half of the water and simmer until you have a nice colour, then turn into the rhubarb, and leave all to mash for 14 days. Then strain, throwing the pulp away.

3. Put the sugar into the liquid, stir until it is dissolved and let it ferment for 14 days. Then skim and bottle. Keep 6 months.

RHUBARB-TOMATO WINE
(This is a grand tonic)

Ingredients :

6 lbs. rhubarb
4 lbs. tomatoes
4½ lbs. sugar
1 gallon water

Method :

1. Cut up the rhubarb small, cover with cold water Add the tomatoes and stand 14 days, stirring and squeezing the tomatoes every day.

2. Strain and put the sugar into the liquid, stirring until it is dissolved. Let it ferment 14 days then strain and bottle, corking lightly.

RHUBARB-WALLFLOWER PORT

Ingredients :

>6 lbs. rhubarb
>1 gallon cold water
>4 lbs. sugar
>1 pint of blood red wallflower petals (no green must be used)

Method :

1. Cut up the rhubarb small and cover with cold water. Leave to mash 1 week, stirring every day. Then add (pressed down) 1 pint red wallflower petals. Leave to mash a further 3 days then strain and throw away all the pulp.

2. Add the sugar and stir until dissolved. Leave to ferment 14 days, then skim and bottle.

3. Wallflower petals give a heat-like good spirit to the brew. The red gives a purple hue to the wine. No green must go in because it is very harsh.

RHUBARB-WALLFLOWER WINE

Ingredients :

>6 lbs. rhubarb
>1 gallon water
>1 pint yellow wallflower petals (no green must be used)
>4 lbs. sugar

Method :

1. Cut up the rhubarb small and cover with the cold water. Leave to mash one week, stirring every day, then add 1 pint (pressed down) of yellow wallflowers. Leave to mash a further 3 days, then strain and throw away all the pulp.

2. Add the sugar and stir until it is dissolved. Leave it to ferment 14 days then skim and bottle. Keep 6 months.

RHUBARB WINE (1)

Ingredients :

>5 lbs. chopped rhubarb
>1 gallon cold water
>Yellow rind of 1 lemon
>4 lbs. sugar
>½ oz. isinglass

Method :

1. Cover the rhubarb with water and allow to stand 5 days, then strain out the pulp, and squeeze all the moisture out of it before throwing it away.

2. Add the sugar to the liquid and thin yellow rind of lemon and isinglass. Stir until the sugar is dissolved and leave to ferment for 14 days, then skim and bottle and keep 12 months. A delicious light wine.

RHUBARB WINE (2)

Ingredients :

>5 lbs. rhubarb
>1 gallon cold water
>4 lbs. sugar
>1 lb. large raisins
>1 oz. yeast
>½ pint sherry (this is optional as the wine is quite good and rich without it)

Method:

1. Cut the rhubarb small and cover with cold water. Stir often and leave to stand 14 days. Squeeze the rhubarb.

2. Add the sugar and chopped raisins, stir until the sugar is dissolved, then sprinkle the yeast on top. Let it ferment 8 days, then strain and add the sherry and bottle—corking lightly.

3. By keeping 12 months this develops an unbelievable body.

RHUBARB WINE (3)

Ingredients :

>5 lbs. rhubarb
>1 gallon cold water
>3½ lbs. white sugar
>The juice only of 1½ lemons

Method :

1. Cut up the rhubarb very small and cover with the cold water. Stir often and stand 8 days, then squeeze all the goodness out of the pulp before throwing it away.

2. Stir in the sugar and lemon juice and stand the liquid in a warm room to ferment. Skim and leave until no more scum arises. Then strain and bottle, corking lightly.

3. A fine light golden wine.

RHUBARB WINE (4)
(Double strength)

Ingredients :

>2 gallons rhubarb
>1 gallon water
>5 lbs. sugar

Method :

1. Cut up one gallon of rhubarb very small, put it in a bowl and cover with cold water. Leave 7 days stirring often, then squeeze out of the liquid all the rhubarb pulp.

2. Now add the second gallon of rhubarb, cut up very fine and put it into the liquid. Stir often and leave 7 more days, then squeeze out all the pulp.

3. Add the sugar to the liquid and stir it away. Leave to ferment for 14 days, then skim and bottle.

RICE WINE

Ingredients :

    3 lbs. rice
    3 lbs. sugar
    1 lb. large raisins
    1 oz. yeast
    1 gallon water
    A pinch of isinglass

Method :

1. Put the rice and sugar into a bowl, cover with warm water. Add the chopped raisins and dissolve the yeast in a little warm water and add. Put the isinglass over the top.

2. Stir often the first 3 days, then leave to ferment.

3. Leave 9 days in all before straining and bottling.

ROWANBERRY WINE (1)

Ingredients :

    ½ gallon ripe rowanberries
    1 gallon boiling water
    3½ lbs. white sugar

Method :

1. Strip the berries from the stems and pour the boiling water over them. Let it stand 6 days, stirring and squeezing daily, then strain.

2. Add the sugar to the liquid and stir until it is perfectly dissolved.

3. Set in a warm place and let it ferment 16 days, then skim and bottle.

ROWANBERRY WINE (2)

Ingredients :

> 1 gallon of rowanberries
> 1 gallon water
> 4 lbs. sugar
> ½ lb. wheat
> 1 oz. yeast
> 1 oz. whole ginger
> 1 tablespoonful raisins

Method :

1. Pour the boiling water over the berries and let them stand 4 days, then strain.

2. Put the sugar, chopped raisins and wheat into the liquid and stir until the sugar is dissolved, then when lukewarm sprinkle the yeast on top and add the well bruised ginger. Leave to ferment 16 days then skim, strain and bottle.

SAFFRON WINE

Ingredients :

> 1 gallon rhubarb
> 1 gallon water
> 4 lbs. sugar
> Big pinch of saffron (or if in liquid form a tablespoonful)
> 1 lb. wheat
> ½ lb. raisins
> ½ oz. yeast

Method :

1. Cut the rhubarb up and cover with the water. Leave 14 days, stirring every day, then squeeze the rhubarb out.

2. Add the sugar to the liquid and stir until it is dissolved, then add the saffron, chopped raisins and wheat. Sprinkle the yeast on top and leave to ferment 16 days.

3. Then skim, strain and bottle.
This is a blood purifier and tonic.

SAGE WINE

Ingredients :

> As many young sage leaves as will fill a pint pot—well
> pressed down
> 1 gallon rhubarb
> 4 lbs. sugar
> 1 lb. large raisins
> 1 gallon hot water

Method :

1. Cut the rhubarb up small and roughly chop the sage. Put in a bowl with the chopped raisins.

2. Pour the hot water over and stir daily for 14 days, then strain and squeeze all moisture from the pulp before throwing it away.

3. Add the sugar to the liquid and stir until it is dissolved, then leave to ferment 14 days, before skimming and bottling the brew.

A larger quantity of sage may be added if the flavour is liked.

SLOE WINE

Ingredients :

> 1 gallon sloes
> 1 gallon boiling water
> 4 lbs. sugar
> 1 oz. yeast

Method :

1. Put the sloes in a dish and cover with the boiling water. Leave for 14 days, squeezing the fruit and stirring all up each day, then strain.

2. Put the sugar in the liquid and stir until it is dissolved then sprinkle the yeast on top and put in a warm place to ferment.

3. Leave one month then skim and bottle.

STRAWBERRY WINE (1)

Ingredients :

1 gallon ripe strawberries
1 gallon water
3½ lbs. white sugar
¼ lb. large raisins
1 oz. yeast; 1 large slice of toast

Method :

1. Hull the strawberries and put them in the preserving pan with the water and simmer gently for 15 minutes after bringing to the boil.

2. Strain and add the sugar and stir until it is dissolved. Add the raisins (pulled apart) and the yeast spread on the toast and leave to ferment 8 days. Then skim and bottle.

3. This is a fine wine but needs keeping to mature.

STRAWBERRY WINE (2)

Ingredients :

1 gallon ripe strawberries
2 lbs. red cherries
4 lbs. white sugar
1 lb. wheat
1 oz. yeast
1 gallon cold water

Method :

1. Stand the fruit and water in a large bowl, squeezing the fruit every day. Add the sugar, wheat and yeast— stir up often—pushing the fruit down among the liquid. Leave 21 days.

2. Then strain and bottle.

Point to remember : You must stir it 2 or 3 times a day or it will mould—and too much of it will spoil the flavour.

SULTANA WINE
(Gingered)

Ingredients :

> 1 oz. whole ginger
> 1 gallon warm water
> 2 lbs. sultanas
> 1 lb. wheat
> 3½ lbs. sugar
> Juice and rind of 1 lemon
> 1 oz. yeast

Method :

1. Mince the sultanas, bruise the ginger well, put into a bowl with the wheat and juice and rind of lemon. Cover with the water.

2. Add the sugar and stir the yeast in. Let it stand 21 days, stirring often, then strain.

3. Let it stand 14 days, then bottle, corking loosely.

SWEETHEART WINE

Ingredients :

> 6 lbs. apples
> 6 large Jaffa oranges
> 4 lbs. sugar
> 1 gallon water

Method :

1. Cut the apples up small. Peel off the orange skin as whole as possible and add it to the apples. Slice the oranges, pour over the water and leave 4 days.

2. Add the sugar and leave to ferment 1 month, squeezing the oranges and apples daily, but take the whole skins out on the 10th day and on no account squeeze them.

3. Then strain and bottle. On no account squeeze the orange skins or the wine will be very bitter.

TOMATO WINE

Ingredients :

8 lbs. ripe tomatoes
1 gallon water
1 tablespoonful salt
3½ lbs. sugar
1 oz. whole ginger
1 oz. yeast; 1 slice toast

Method :

1. Boil the sugar and ginger which has been well bruised, with the water for 20 minutes.

2. Then turn it boiling on to the tomatoes and salt. When lukewarm add the yeast spread on both sides of the toast, float in the liquid and leave to ferment 21 days, squeezing the tomatoes daily.

3. Then strain and stand 3 weeks before bottling.
This is a grand pick-me-up.

TONIC WINE (1)

Ingredients :

6 lbs. beetroots
3 lbs. Demerara sugar
½ pint Guinness's Stout

Method :

1. Wash the beetroots and cut them into thin slices in a bowl. Sprinkle the sugar over the slices.

2. Leave for 2 days then strain off all the liquid and mix it with the stout. Bottle and cork tightly.

3. Take a tablespoonful 3 times a day.
A recognised cure for anaemia.

TONIC WINE (2)

Ingredients:

>   1 glass rum
>   A small jar of beef extract
>   ½ lb. Demerara sugar
>   ¼ pint black beer
>   1 pint of Old Tom

Method :

1. Mix altogether and take a wine glass once daily.

VANILLA WINE

Ingredients :

>   6 lbs. rhubarb
>   1 gallon May flowers (Hawthorn)
>   4 lbs. sugar
>   1 gallon water
>   2 lemons

Method :

1. Cut the rhubarb up small, cover with cold water and add the hawthorn blossoms and lemons cut in slices. Stir daily for 14 days.

2. Strain and add the sugar. Stir until it is dissolved then leave to ferment 1 week.

3. Then skim, strain and bottle, keeping 8 months to mature.

VINE LEAVES WINE

Ingredients :

> 5 lbs. leaves and stems
> 1 gallon boiling water
> 3½ lbs. sugar

Method :

1. Put the leaves in a bowl and pour the boiling water over. Let it stand 3 days, then squeeze the leaves and stems out of the liquid.

2. Put the sugar into the liquid and stir until dissolved, then let it ferment for 10 days.

3. Skim, strain and bottle.

When the vines have to be pruned the young fresh leaves and stems are full of flavour.

WALNUT WINE

Ingredients :

> 1 large bouquet of walnut leaves
> 1 gallon water
> 3 lbs. sugar
> ½ lb. raisins
> 1 oz. yeast ; 1 slice of toast

Method :

1. Boil the sugar and water together and pour over the walnut leaves. Stand 24 hours then squeeze out the leaves.

2. Add the chopped raisins and diced toast to the liquid and sprinkle the yeast on top. Leave to ferment 24 days, then strain and bottle.

WHEAT WINE

Ingredients :

  1 lb. wheat
  2 lbs. sultanas (chopped)
  1 lb. old potatoes (chopped finely)
  4 lbs. sugar
  1 oz. yeast
  1 gallon hot water
  2 grape fruits

Method :

1. Put the wheat, sultanas, potatoes, sugar and juice and rinds of grape fruit into a bowl.

2. Pour the hot water over and stir until the sugar is dissolved.

3. Sprinkle the yeast in when it cools to lukewarm and leave to ferment 21 days.

4. Then strain and bottle.

WHIN WINE

Ingredients :

  ½ gallon whin blooms
  1 gallon hot water
  1 lemon
  2 lbs. sugar
  1 lb. raisins
  1 large slice toast ; 1 oz. yeast

Method :

1. Put blooms, water and sugar in a bowl and leave for a week. Every day push the blooms down and stir well, then strain the blooms out.

2. Add the chopped lemon and raisins to the liquid and spread the yeast on both sides of the toast and float on top. Leave 14 days.

3. Then skim, strain and bottle.

Gather the yellow whin flowers on a dry day. (In some parts this is called Gorse.)

WHITE CURRANT WINE

Ingredients :

1 gallon white currants
1 gallon boiling water
1 lb. large raisins
3¾ lb. white sugar

Method :

1. Put the currants into a bowl. (I generally rip them off the strap.) Add the chopped raisins, sugar and boiling water.

2. Stir and mash the fruit every day for 14 days.

3. Then strain and squeeze all the moisture from the pulp which you throw away.

4. Then strain the liquid twice and bottle.

YARROW SHERRY

Ingredients :

1 gallon boiling water
2 quarts yarrow flowers
4 lbs. white sugar
Rind and juice of 4 lemons
1 cake of shredded wheat
1 oz. yeast ; 1 slice of toast

Method :

1. Pour the water over the flowers and leave 4 or 5 days, then strain.

2. Boil the liquid with the sugar for 20 minutes, then pour it over the sliced lemons and leave until lukewarm.

3. Then add the shredded wheat crumbled up and the yeast spread on toast. Let it ferment for 21 days, then skim and bottle.

YARROW WINE

Ingredients :

 1 gallon boiling water
 3 quarts yarrow flowers
 4 lbs. white sugar
 Rind and juice of 4 oranges
 1 oz. yeast ; 1 large slice of toast

Method :

1. Pour the water over the flowers and leave to soak 4 or 5 days, then strain.

2. Put the liquid into a pan with the sugar and thinly peeled rind of the oranges and simmer 20 minutes.

3. Slice the oranges into the bowl and pour the liquid over then allow to cool to lukewarm.

4. Spread the yeast on toast and float in the liquid and leave to ferment for 14 days, then skim and bottle.

YELLOW RASPBERRY WINE

Ingredients :

 1 gallon yellow raspberries
 1 gallon warm water
 4 lbs. Demerara sugar

Method :

1. Put the raspberries into a bowl and pour the hot water over. Add the sugar and stir, squeezing the fruit well until the sugar is dissolved.

2. Keep squeezing and stirring every day for 14 days, then strain and stand the liquid in a jar for 1 week.

3. Then pour off the clear liquid into bottles.

RECIPES FOR BEERS, MINERALS, ETC.

APPLE BEER

Ingredients :

> 4 lbs. apples
> 2 gallons cold water
> 3 lbs. sugar
> 2 ozs. whole ginger
> 1 teaspoonful cloves
> 1 teaspoonful cinnamon

Method :

1. Grate the apples up with a suet grater and put them in a bowl with the cold water. Stir every day for a week then strain.

2. Add the sugar, cloves, cinnamon and ginger (well bruised). Stir well and leave overnight.

3. Then strain and bottle, cork lightly for a week, then it is ready for use and tastes delicious.

BEETROOT COCKTAIL

Ingredients :

4 lbs. beetroot
1 gallon water
¼ oz. hops
½ lb. malt
4 lbs. sugar
1 oz. yeast
1 large slice of toast

Method :

1. Divide the water into three parts.

2. Clean and cut up the beetroot and place in one portion of water. Boil together gently for 20 minutes then strain the beetroot out.

3. Boil the hops in the second portion of water for 30 minutes then strain the hops out.

4. If the malt is the dry corn kind, it must be boiled for 30 minutes in the remaining portion of water. If the liquid jelly-like kind, it only needs stirring away in hot water.

5. Put all the three liquids together and measure it. Make it up to the gallon.

6. Add the sugar and stir until it is dissolved. When lukewarm add the yeast spread on toast.

7. Let it ferment 21 days then skim and bottle, corking loosely until fermentation ceases.

8. When the harsh period is over pour off the clear wine from the sediment that will fall to the bottom of the bottles.

This was like whisky, brandy and rum mixed and slightly sweetened.

BLACKCURRANT GIN

Ingredients :

> 1½ pints gin
> Large heaped breakfastcupful of large, ripe, juicy black-
> currants
> A scant third of a cup of sugar

Method :

1. Pick stalks off blackcurrants and add them with the sugar to the gin.

2. Shake every day until the blackcurrants are but a fine sediment in the bottom of the bottle, then strain.

3. Taste, and add more sugar if needed to suit your taste.

BLACK ROB

(For breaking up a cold)

Ingredients :

> 3 pints blackcurrant juice
> 3 lbs. sugar
> ½ oz. whole cloves
> ½ oz. cassia buds
> ½ oz. whole white ginger

Method :

1. Extract the juice by heating a vessel containing very ripe blackcurrants in a pan of boiling water—the heat makes the juice run—and it is easily strained off.

2. Put the juice, sugar, cloves, cassia and ginger (well bruised) into a pan. Bring slowly to the boil, stirring to dissolve the sugar, then boil a full 5 minutes by the clock. Add a glass of brandy and bottle.

3. A measure with boiling water is an excellent cold cure.

BRAMBLE VINEGAR
(Strong and Rich)

Ingredients :

3 lbs. brambles
1 quart white wine vinegar
Allow 1 lb. sugar to 1 pint of juice

Method :

1. Pick over the brambles and cover them with the vinegar. Allow to stand 8 days, stirring often, then strain through muslin.

2. Measure the juice and allow 1 lb. of sugar to each pint. Put in a pan, bring to the boil and simmer gently for 5 minutes, then bottle and cork well.

You must be careful in boiling to time or it will jelly.

A measure of this is delightful in cold water as a refreshing drink on a hot summer's day or with hot water as a night cap for a cold.

CARROT WHISKY

Ingredients :

6 lbs. carrots
1 gallon water
4 lbs. sugar
A tablespoonful raisins
1 lb. wheat
1 oz. yeast
2 lemons
2 oranges

Method :

1. Wash the carrots well, but do not peel. Put into the water and bring to the boil then simmer gently until the carrots are very tender. Use the carrots for food, and strain the water.

2. Into a bowl put the sugar, sliced oranges and lemons and pour over the hot liquid. Stir until the sugar is dissolved and then stand until lukewarm.

3. Then add the chopped raisins, wheat and sprinkle the yeast on the top. Leave to ferment 15 days.

4. Then skim, strain and bottle. Keep almost a year.

DAISY WHISKY

Ingredients :

> 4 quarts of the small field daisy blossoms
> 1 gallon boiling water
> 1 lb. wheat
> 1 lb. large raisins
> 2 lemons
> 2 oranges
> 3½ lbs. sugar
> 1 oz. yeast

Method :

1. Put the daisies in a bowl and cover with the boiling water. Stand until next day then squeeze the daisies out.

2. Slice the oranges and lemons into the liquid and add the sugar and stir until it is dissolved. Leave until lukewarm.

3. Then add the chopped raisins, wheat and sprinkle the yeast on top. Leave for 21 days to ferment.

4. Then skim, strain and bottle. Keep 6 months.

DAMSON GIN

Ingredients :

> 2 lbs. damsons
> 1 quart gin
> 1 lb. brown sugar candy or lump sugar—or barley sugar
>   will do

Method :

1. Prick all the damsons with a needle and crush the candy.

2. Put in a big bottle or jar and add the gin. Shake often for 2 months.

3. Then strain and bottle. The longer it is kept the better.

ELDERFLOWER LEMONADE

Ingredients :

    1 pint elderflowers
    1 gallon of water
    1 lemon
    1½ lbs. loaf sugar
    2 tablespoonfuls white wine vinegar

Method :

1. Put all in a bowl adding the lemon cut in four. Let it infuse for 24 hours, stirring often and giving the lemon a slight squeeze.

2. Then strain and bottle, tying the corks in securely, and lay the bottles on their sides.

FRUIT SYRUPS

Choice of Fruits :

    Raspberry, Strawberry, Bramble, Red, Black and White Currant, Loganberry, Victoria Plum, Blaeberry, Cranberry and Cherry. Take the stones from the plum and cherry.

Method :

1. Put the fruit in a large jar and stand the jar in a pan of boiling water until all the juice is given off, then strain off the juice and when the fruit has cooled enough to handle, squeeze it through a muslin. Add this juice to the rest and strain all of it again. Throw the pulp away.

2. Measure the juice and allow a pound of white sugar to every pint of juice.

3. Put juice and sugar into the pan and bring to the boil, taking care to stir the sugar away, skimming as the scum arises.

4. After it comes to the boil, boil 5 minutes by the clock and then allow to cool.

5. Stir into each quart of syrup half pint brandy and bottle, corking well.

A measure of these in plain water or soda water is an excellent summer drink. In hot water an excellent night cap for a cold.

Mixed in a shaker with a little spirit such as gin—an excellent cocktail.

GINGER BEER
(Urpeth)

Ingredients :

$\frac{1}{2}$ oz. tartaric acid
$\frac{1}{2}$ oz. cream of tartar
$\frac{1}{2}$ oz. essence of ginger
2 lbs. of sugar
1 oz. yeast
and almost 2 gallons of water

Method :

1. Put tartaric acid, cream of tartar, ginger essence and sugar into a bowl and pour over 1 gallon of boiling water. Stir until ingredients are dissolved and add a gallon or so of cold water until lukewarm.

2. Then add yeast mixed with a tablespoonful of sugar. Let it stand until cold.

3. Bottle and tie up securely. Screw tops are best. Enough to make 20 pint bottles.

GLEN IRIS HOP BITTERS

Ingredients :

3 ozs. hops
1 oz. whole ginger (well bruised)
2 lbs. brown sugar
3 gallons water
1 oz. yeast and a little honey

Method :

1. Boil hops, ginger and sugar in 2 quarts of water gently for $2\frac{1}{2}$ hours, then strain.

2. Then add water to make 3 gallons. Stir away a little honey and sprinkle the yeast in, giving it a good stir.

3. Stand till cold then bottle.

Point to remember : Beer must be lukewarm when the yeast is added.

HOME BREWED STOUT

Ingredients :

3½ gallons of water
1½ lbs. of black malt
1½ ozs. of hops
½ oz. yeast
1 lb. brown sugar
2 oz. black spanish

Method :

1. Stir the malt away in the boiling water, add the hops and boil for 30 minutes.

2. Strain on to the sugar and stir until dissolved. When lukewarm, stir in the yeast and ferment for 24 hours, skimming frequently.

3. Pour off carefully leaving the dregs. Bottle and cork tightly.

4. The stout should be ready for use in 4 or 5 days. It improves with keeping.

A point to remember : The malt can be bought at a chemist's in treacle form.

HONEY BOTCHARD

Ingredients :

1 oz. hops
3½ lbs. honey
1 gallon water
1 oz. yeast
1 slice of toast

Method :

1. Boil the hops in the water for 30 minutes then strain.

2. Stir the honey into the liquid. Spread the yeast on both sides of the toast and float it in the wine and leave to ferment for 21 days. Then skim and bottle.

Yorkshire folk swear by brewer's yeast for making the finest Honey Botchard.

HOP BEER

Ingredients :

¼ lb. hops
3 lbs. sugar
½ oz. bruised ginger
2 ozs. yeast
1 tablespoonful of cracked maize
3½ gallons water

Method :

1. Put the cracked maize with the hops and bruised ginger into a bag of butter muslin.

2. Place in 3½ gallons of water and boil until the bag sinks. Lift out the bag, stir in sugar and boil for 5 minutes and strain.

3. When lukewarm add yeast spread on a slice of burnt toast. Stand for three days, bottle and tie securely. It will be ready in a fortnight and it keeps well for weeks.

4. Cracked maize can be bought at the poultry food shop.

LEMON GINGER BEER
(For Haytime)

Ingredients :

3 lbs. sugar
2 ozs. whole ginger
2 ozs. cream of tartar
3 lemons
1 oz. yeast
2 gallons boiling water

Method :

1. Peel the lemon rinds thinly and squeeze out the juice. Put with the sugar, bruised ginger and cream of tartar in a big jar and pour over 2 gallons of boiling water.

2. When lukewarm mix the yeast with a little of the beer and spread it over a slice of toast and lay it on top of the brew. Let it ferment 24 hours, then strain and bottle, corking securely.

ORANGE GIN
(Littlethorpe)

Ingredients :

Six Seville oranges
2½ lemons
1½ lbs. loaf sugar
3 bottles of best unsweetened gin

Method :

1. Peel the fruit thinly (that is just taking off the yellow rind) and put peel, sugar and gin into a jar.

2. Shake up each day for 14 days then strain and bottle.

PARSLEY BRANDY

Ingredients :

½ lb. parsley
1 gallon water
3½ lbs. sugar
2 oranges
2 lemons
½ oz. yeast
1 slice toast
½ oz. white lump ginger
Raisins

Method :

1. Wash the parsley and add it to the water and boil it for 30 minutes, then strain and throw the parsley away.

2. Halve the oranges, and lemons, and put with the sugar and lump ginger well bruised in a bowl. Pour the boiling liquid on and stir until sugar is dissolved.

3. When lukewarm add the yeast spread on toast. After 7 days skim and bottle. Put two large juicy raisins, pulled apart, into each bottle.

RASPBERRY VINEGAR

Ingredients :

> 1 quart vinegar
> 1 quart raspberries
> To each pint of juice 1 lb. white sugar

Method :

1. Put the vinegar in a bowl and add the raspberries as you gather them (if you just have a few bushes) until you have one quart.

2. Squeeze and mash every day for 9 days, then squeeze all through a muslin, and strain again.

3. Measure, add the sugar and bring to the boil and then boil only 5 minutes by the clock.

4. Fine on rice or plain suet pudding and for a summer's drink with cold water. With hot water a fine remedy for a cold.

RED ROB

Ingredients :

> Ripe elderberries
> Water
> To every pint of juice 1 lb. sugar
> To 3 pints allow ½ oz. cassia buds, ½ oz. whole white ginger and ½ oz. whole cloves

Method :

1. Strip the elderberries from the stalks and cover them with water and simmer for 20 minutes until all the juice is in the water, then strain.

2. Measure, add the sugar, cassia, ginger (well bruised) and cloves, and boil all together 10 minutes. You must be careful or it will jelly. A measure in hot water is a fine night cap for a cold.

RHUBARB-APRICOT WHISKY

Ingredients :

> 1 gallon of rhubarb
> 2 lbs. dried apricots
> 1 gallon water
> 4 lbs. sugar
> 1 oz. yeast on a large slice of toast

Method :

1. Soak the apricots in the cold water overnight then boil them gently until very tender. Strain from the water and use the apricots.

2. Cut up the rhubarb and add it to the apricot water which must be made up to 1 gallon. Leave 14 days, stirring often, then strain.

3. Add the sugar to the strained liquid and stir until it is dissolved, then add the yeast spread on the toast. Let it ferment 10 days, skim and bottle. Keep 6 months

RHUBARB BAKE WHISKY

Ingredients :

> 1 lb. bread
> 1 gallon rhubarb
> 1 gallon water
> 4 lbs. sugar
> ½ oz. yeast

Method :

1. Cut the bread into slices and toast it a nice brown both sides—but on no account burn or this spoils the flavour entirely.

2. Put in a bowl, cover with the cold water. Cut the rhubarb up and add. Leave to mash for 9 days, stirring often and squeezing the toast up with the hand, then strain and throw away the pulp.

3. Add the sugar and stir until it is dissolved, then sprinkle the dry yeast over the top. Let it ferment 14 days then skim and bottle.

RHUBARB BRANDY
(A White Wine)

Ingredients :

> 6 lbs. rhubarb
> 1 gallon cold water
> ½ lb. large raisins
> 4 egg shells
> 4 lbs. white sugar

Method :

1. Peel all the green and red off the rhubarb then cut it up small and weigh. Put in a bowl, cover with the water and add the raisins, roughly chopped. Allow to stand a fortnight, stirring and squeezing the rhubarb and raisins every day. Strain and throw away the pulp.

2. Add the sugar and egg shells, crushed to pieces, to the liquid. Then allow to ferment 8 days before taking the scum off. Bottle and cork lightly.

RHUBARB COCKTAIL
(A Fine Rich Wine)

Ingredients :

> 2 lbs. mixed dried fruit
> 2 gallons rhubarb
> 1 gallon water
> 5 lbs. sugar

Method :

1. Soak the fruit in the water overnight then bring to the boil and simmer until tender. Strain out the fruit and use as food. Make the water up to 1 gallon.

2. Cut up 1 gallon of rhubarb and put it in the fruit water. Stir often and leave to stand 1 week. Squeeze out all the rhubarb pulp and cut up and add a further gallon of rhubarb. Let it stand another week then squeeze all the pulp out.

3. Add the sugar, stir until dissolved. Allow to ferment 14 days then skim and bottle.

RHUBARB WHISKY (1)

Ingredients :

1 gallon rhubarb
1 gallon cold water
4 lbs. Demerara sugar
4 lemons
1½ lbs. clean wheat
½ lb. raisins
1 oz. yeast
2 egg shells

Method :

1. Cut the rhubarb up small and cover it with cold water. Add the wheat and leave to mash for 14 days, stirring often. Strain and squeeze all the moisture out of the pulp before throwing it away.

2. Strain the liquid through 3 thicknesses of flannel and add the sugar, thinly pared yellow rind and juice of the lemons, chopped raisins and crushed egg shells, sprinkle the yeast on top and put in a warm place to ferment. After 12 days skim and bottle; it matures in 6 months.

Point to remember: It ferments a long time in a cloudy condition.

RHUBARB WHISKY (2)

Ingredients :

25 lbs. rhubarb
11 lbs. sugar
5 lemons
3½ gallons water
1 lb. large raisins
The shells of 3 eggs

Method :

1. Cut up the rhubarb small and cover with cold water. Stand for 14 days, stirring twice daily, then drain off the liquid and knead and press the rhubarb to get all the juice out.

2. Add the raisins, egg shells (well crushed), lemon juice and the yellow rind grated, stirring well. Let it ferment for 4 days before touching it ; after that each day take off the scum until no scum is left, then leave for 3 weeks before putting into bottles.

3. This is good and a nice quantity for those who have big enough utensils.

SLOE GIN

(Alnwick)

Ingredients :

4 quarts ripe sloes
4 quarts unsweetened gin
3 lbs. crushed sugar candy (brown)
1 oz. bitter almonds
12 cloves

Method :

1. Prick the sloes all over with a silver-plated fork.

2. Put them into a large jar or bottle, add the sugar candy, gin, cloves and sliced almonds.

3. Shake it every day for a month then occasionally for another month.

4. Then strain and bottle.

STRAWBERRY VINEGAR

Ingredients :

> 1 quart ripe strawberries
> 1 quart white vinegar
> To every pint of juice 1 lb. white sugar

Method :

1. Cover the strawberries with the vinegar and let them stand 6 days, while you press and squeeze them daily. Then strain off the juice.

2. Measure and add the sugar then bring to the boil and boil 5 minutes. You must be careful to time the boiling or the vinegar will jelly.

TONIC STOUT

Ingredients :

> 7 lbs. parsnips
> 2 gallons water
> ¼ lb. hops
> ½ lb. brown malt (such as is bought in treacle form at the chemist's)
> 4 lbs. sugar
> 1 oz. yeast

Method :

1. Clean and boil the parsnips in 1 gallon of water until the parsnips are tender (do not peel them). Strain the water.

2. Boil the hops in 1 gallon of water for ¼ hour, then strain.

3. Add the two waters together, stir away in it the sugar and malt and leave until lukewarm.

4. Sprinkle the yeast on top and leave 2 days, then bottle. Do not cork tightly or you will have explosions.